FIX IT FAST & EASY! 2
UPGRADING YOUR HOUSE

Glenn Haege

Edited by Kathy Stief
Illustrated by Ken Taylor
Cover Photo by David A. Frechette

D1407766

MASTER HANDYMAN PRESS, INC.

1

FIX IT FAST & EASY! 2
UPGRADING YOUR HOUSE

Glenn Haege

Edited by Kathy Stief

Published by:
  Master Handyman Press, Inc.
  Post Office Box 1498
  Royal Oak, MI 48068-1498 USA

First Printing January 1998

Printed in the United States of America

Library of Congress Cataloging in Publication Data.
Haege, Glenn
  Upgrading your home
  Bibliography: h.

ISBN 1-880615-06-1

To my Mom and Dad,
Robert and Marion Haege.
You always supported
my ideas, wishes and wants.
Now I can thank you
for making me do my homework.

Acknowledgments

This book has taken twice as long as it was supposed to because my life has been filled with wonderful distractions. Both my editor, Kathy, and I had weddings in our families. Mel Karmazan of CBS said the magic words and my "Ask the Handyman" radio show was syndicated on close to 150 radio stations by Westwood One.

In between, I wrote this book. The subject is so broad, I called in friends from throughout the modernization, building materials, and hardware industries, to make certain the information was as up to the minute as possible.

I'll take full credit for all the mistakes, but have to share credit for the "good stuff" with the pros who helped me. Here are the names of just a few: Al King, Atlas Fireplaces; Don Collins, Budget Electric; Nancy Rosen, Builders Association of SE Michigan; Tom Roncelli, Century 21 - Royale; Mike McCoy, Coy Construction; Sandy Cornillie, J. C. Cornillie; Bill Damman, Damman Hardware; Doug Beauvais, Data Reproductions; John Finely, Diversified Energy Control, LTD; Jerry Goetz and Bill Steel, Detroit Edison; Gary Marowske, Flame Furnace; Adam Helfman, Fairway Construction; Murray Gula, Michigan Construction Protection Agency; Pat Murphy, Pat Murphy, Inc.; Nelson Wood, N. A. Mans; Joe Aielo, Pine Building; Mike Palazzolo, Safety King; Connie Morebach, Sanit Air; Jim Kronk, Universal Plumbing; Jim Williams, William's Refrigeration.

I'm sure I missed somebody, but don't worry guys, I'll get to you in the next book.

My editor, Kathy Stief, should be a midwife in her next life. She literally pulled this book out of me. Wife, Barbara, and daughter, Heather, both broke their previous world records for number of one liners and zingers delivered while proof reading a manuscript. Friend and Affiliate Relations Director, Rob David, kept up his proof reading duties even from a hospital bed. As always, artist, Ken Taylor, pulled off minor miracles, and Gordon Sommer took Kathy and my floppy disks and made them look like a book. Amazing!

My biggest "thanks" go to you, the listeners and readers who call and write me every week. In the past fifteen years, I've answered over 40,000 of your questions over the radio.

You tell me what you want to know, what you understand, what I have to say a little more clearly, or in more detail. You, all of you, are the magic ingredients that make my books and shows successful. You make it so easy, all I have to do is answer the questions. Thank you.

Glenn Haege
Royal Oak, Michigan

Table of Contents

Table of Contents

Table of Contents

Table of Contents

Table of Contents

Table of Contents

Chapter	Subject	Page

Table of Contents

Table of Contents

Table of Contents

Table of Contents

Table of Contents

Table of Contents

Introduction

This is the second book in the *Fix It Fast & Easy!* series. It is subtitled **Upgrading Your House** because the major emphasis of the book is on doing the big jobs which can drain the bank account and give any home owner cold sweats in the middle of the night.

Major purchases, such as air conditioning and heating systems, roofing, flooring, insulation, siding and concrete drive ways are included.

Major problems, like sick building syndrome, lead poisoning, water purification, and the bug-a-boo of radon will be explained and solutions offered in *Fix It Fast & Easy! #3, Frantic Fixes*. I wish I had the room to explain it all here, but my editor tells me I've already used too many pages.

My plan is to take you step-by-step through all the big jobs. In addition to my usual question and answer, cook book direction technique to specific "How To" questions, I've included essay length explanations of many of the subjects.

Many of these essays are adapted from articles that first saw the light of day in **TwentyOne Magazine** or in my weekly articles in the **Homestyle Section** of **The Detroit News**. Indeed, it has been the success of these articles, and the hundreds of people who have told me they clip and save all of them, or refer to them on the internet at the *Detroit News* website at www.detnews.com, that convinced me you want easy to understand, in-depth explanations.

The answers you read here are as close to the cutting edge of home remodeling and repair today as I can make them. My editor and I have been working on the book for over three years and have constantly updated the chapters as new information became available.

Future editions will be published as home improvement technology changes and newer, faster, better ways are created for the home handy man and woman to accomplish these major projects.

Not every person is equipped to do every project. I wouldn't climb up a ladder and do a repair on my roof if you paid me my weight in gold (and that would be a lot of gold).

My wife, Barbara, is a far better painter than I will ever be. Even though I am certified, I do not do electrical. Unless a person has great skills, or really enjoys "DIY", I don't believe they should try to install a furnace or build a room addition.

You may be that one in a million who does all these things and more. If you are, I will be very proud to shake your hand, and will gladly stand in line to buy a copy of your book.

This book, my book, is for the rest of us. It is for the men and women who do all they can on nights and weekends, then want to learn what they need to know to be wise consumers on the major projects.

It is for busy professional people, or older people, or single parents, who don't have the time to actually do the projects, but need a quick way to learn enough to make sure the people they consider hiring, actually know what they are talking about; and that once started, the job gets done right.

I've tried to lay out this book logically, so that you can find what you need easily. There are four sections. Section I, You or Who?, deals with who does what, when. Section II, Living Space, covers the modernization of the rooms we live in. Section III, Mechanicals, covers all the things, like the furnace and water heater, that we don't even think about until something goes wrong. Section IV, Protection from the Elements, covers the "wrapping" of the house.

Enough talk. Let's start doing. But, wait a minute, just exactly who, should be doing what? We discuss that very problem in the first few chapters.

WARNING - DISCLAIMER

This book is designed to provide information for the home handy man and woman. it is sold with the understanding that the publisher and author are not engaged in rendering legal, contractor, architectural, or other professional services. If expert assistance is required, the services of competent professionals should be sought.

Every effort has been made to make this text as complete and accurate as possible, and to assure proper credit is given to various contributors and manufacturers, etc.. However, there may be mistakes, both typographical and in content. Therefore, this text should be used only as a general guide and not as the ultimate sourch of information. Furthermore, this book contains information only up to the printing date.

The purpose of this book is to educate and entertain. The author and Master Handyman Press shall have neither liability nor responsibility to any person or entity with respect to any loss or damage caused directly or indirectly by the information contained in this book.

WARNING - DISCLAIMER

Trademark Acknowledgments

Trademarked names, rather than confusion inducing, generic names, are used throughout this book so that readers can ask distributers, retailers, and contractors, about products that interest them. Rather than list the names and entities that own each trademark or insert a trademark symbol with each mention of the trademarked name, the publisher states that it is using the names only for editorial purposes and to the benefit of the trademark owner with no intent of infringing upon that trademark.

Trademark Acknowledgments

Section I:
YOU OR WHO?

DIY or HID? This probably qualifies as one of the great mysteries of life. Should you Do It Yourself or Hire It Done?

We take three chapters to let you find out. The first chapter, oddly enough is titled: DIY or HID? If you read the first paragraph and didn't know what those initials stood for, the matter is already decided. It's HID.

Chapter 2 tells you how to select, live with, hire and fire a contractor.

Chapter 3 tells you how long the job will take and what to expect.

Go get 'em tiger.

Chapter 1
DIY or HID?

DIY or HID?

Do It Yourself, or Hire It Done?

That's the big question. You can do most of the tips I have included in this book yourself. Some of the work will have to be done by a contractor. Deciding what you can, or should do yourself, and what you delegate to others can be a problem. I wrote what I call the Twelve Commandments of DIY to help you decide.

Once you decide you need outside help, hiring a contractor becomes the problem. I've included step by step instructions on how to hire a good contractor in this chapter. Also included are a day by day analysis of how long it takes to plan, organize, and build a job; what you should look for in a good modernization contract; what you should expect when crews start working; and what to do if you are not satisfied with your contractor's performance.

Now come all of you to the mountain top, or at least the top of the roof, and I will give you...

DIY or HID?

The Twelve Commandments of DIY

DIY or HID?

The Twelve Commandments of DIY

I do not mean to be sacrilegious. I didn't really get "The Twelve Commandments of DIY" off a mountain top, but these commandments deserve to be carved in stone.

Follow them and you will never get into trouble on your Do It Yourself projects. Ignore them and your body or your bank book will pay for the oversight.

I Learn all you can before you do.

There is no excuse for not knowing all about a job before starting. Consult my and many other people's books, newspaper and magazine articles, tapes, radio and TV home improvement shows. Get free handouts and attend seminars at paint and hardware stores, home centers, and builders shows.

DIY or HID?

II Plan all jobs well in advance.

Don't try to hire a roofer in the middle of summer, or buy a furnace when the first snow flies. Back time your projects so that you have time to organize, comparison shop, check references, and still be one season ahead of when everybody else is doing that kind of work. Don't stand in line, start the line, and you will get work done by the best professionals at very good prices.

III Always read the directions.

Women are way ahead of the game here. Women read directions and are not afraid to ask. Many men just open a can, box, or bottle, and start working, then wonder why the job goes wrong.

Read directions. Call the company, a buddy, the hardware store, or a radio show like mine, and ask for clarification if everything is not perfectly clear. You will be amazed at how much time and money this saves you.

DIY or HID?

IV Never bite off more than you can chew.

Do It Yourself is one of America's greatest building trends. The more you do, the greater your skills become.

If you become a really good carpenter, go ahead and remodel the kitchen yourself. There will be some "iffy" moments, but you can do it. I can guarantee that you will be an even better carpenter after hanging all those new cabinets and cutting those counter tops.

On the other hand, if you hit your thumb, almost every time you try to hammer a nail, and are proud when you saw a straight line, hire a professional. An amateurish job can cost you many thousands of dollars when it comes time to sell your home. Be smart. Stay within your skill level.

V Never tear up more than one room at a time.

I know that if you are going to paint, it sounds smart to wash the walls in the dining room and family room at the same time. Unfortunately, if we tear up two rooms, the family has no place to go. Mess up one room at a time. Get the job done fast. Clean up right away. And brag about the results.

DIY or HID?

VI Never learn to use a major tool on a big job. Practice on something small.

The use of every major tool, a new saw, a power washer, a paint gun, is a little different. You need to experiment and get the feel of the equipment.

This is especially true with power washers and spray painting equipment. With power washers the tendency is to tear up wood. With spray painting equipment, uneven coverage is the major failing. Either can ruin a job.

VII Never climb a rickety ladder, or any ladder you do not feel comfortable climbing.

Birds fly, People fall and break things. You are not made for bouncing. Cheap, light weight, or rickety ladders have put many people in the hospital.

VIII Never get careless around electrical.

Just brushing against the wrong wire can kill you, or cause you to drop a power tool, or ruin a paint job. Keep yourself, and your ladder away from wiring. Always make certain that the power is turned off before you attempt any electrical repair.

DIY or HID?

IX Never over build for your neighborhood.

"Don't move, improve" is a great slogan and good advice. Just don't go overboard. A 4,000 square foot palace in a cozy neighborhood of 1,200 square foot bungalows will never provide a decent financial return on the dollars invested. If financial return is of prime importance, do not over-build.

X Never be afraid to turn a job over to a professional.

Too many men (thank heavens this is not usually a female failing) have this macho thing, and refuse to believe a job is above their skill level.

My editor's husband ruined three plastic drain repair kits before he gave up and called a plumber. You are too smart for that.

XI Always check references and get a completion date.

Checking references is the only way you can find out if a professional really has the skill to do a job. Putting a completion date in the contract is the only way you can be assured the work will be done on time.

DIY or HID?

Don't sign on the dotted line until you have checked the references and gotten a completion date in writing.

XII Remember, your check book is the most important tool in your tool box.

The power of a checkbook is an awesome thing. Use it properly and it can build you the home of your dreams. Waste it and you will be a very dissatisfied customer.

Now that we've got the ground rules set, and you've made the decision as to when, and when not, to hire a contractor, you have to decide on how to get a good contractor, and what to do once you've got one. Follow the simple rules in the next chapter and you'll get a good contractor every time.

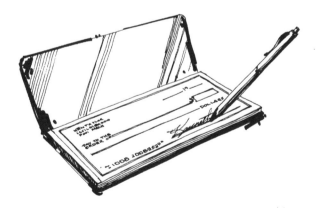

DIY or HID?

Chapter 2
Living with a Contractor

Living with a Contractor
How To Find & Hire a Good Contractor

Every Spring, handymen, trades, and building contractors sprout up like dandelions. The vast majority of them are honest, hard working men and women. Unfortunately a few use shady business tactics to fleece thousands of trusting homeowners, especially women and senior citizens, out of millions of dollars.

Not all damage is done by criminals. Many would-be builders don't know what they are doing. Your bank account can not make a distinction between being fleeced by a criminal or mugged by criminal incompetence. You're out the money either way. Use these few hints to pick a good contractor or tradesman.

When someone solicits to do repairs on your home, you do not know who they are. Take their name, company name, address, phone number, and builder's license number. If you live in a regulated state like Michigan, do not even talk to anyone who cannot show you a valid Builder's or Home Improvement Sales License, complete with Builder's License number and the name of the "qualifying officer" of the firm.

If they say they are working for a nearby home-owner, get the name, address and phone number of that person. Call the person before sitting down for an appoint-

Living with a Contractor

ment. If they don't check out, call the police. Your call could save a neighbor thousands of dollars.

Always get quotes from at least three organizations for any major job. To get the names of good people, ask the folks who man the contract trade counters at wholesalers, lumberyards and home centers for referrals. They like to recommend good customers. The best time to talk to counter people is late in the morning or mid-day.

If a broad choice of quality materials is important, make sure to seek out referrals from wholesalers as well as home centers and lumber yards. Wholesalers offer a wider selection of materials for specific types of jobs, like roofing, siding, ceramic tile, plumbing, and lighting. They get the majority of the top end business.

While you're there, get a feel for the materials that will be used on your job and pick up some brochures. When you get back home, write a thorough description of what you want done. If you wish specific materials, specify them. List manufacturer, trade name, model name and number.

Telephone Quotes

Never take quotes over the telephone. Set appointments in your home. When making the appointments, tell your phone contact that you want the names, addresses and telephone numbers of a minimum of five people who have gotten the same type of job.

Living with a Contractor

Sales Appointments

When the contractor or sales person arrives for their appointment, tell them you will not sign any agreement until after you have contacted and inspected their references.

References, References, References!

Getting and checking references is vital to the shopping process. You want the names, when the job was completed, type of job, address, and telephone number. In addition, some jobs require specific information from references. I'll go into detail about the job specific questions you should ask in the chapter that covers that type of modernization.

The bigger the job, the more references you need. If you are having a deck built, five is plenty. If you are having a major renovation or room addition, it is best to get ten.

Generally, you want one or two current jobs, hopefully something the contractor is working on right now, so you can look at the building site. You also want references on jobs that were completed one, two, and at least five years ago. These are the references that can tell you how

Living with a Contractor

the contractor stands behind his jobs, and how his constructions stands the test of time.

Always ask for job specific references. If you are getting a deck, you want deck references. If you are getting bay windows, you want bay window references. If you are getting a room addition or kitchen renovation, you want room addition or kitchen references.

When checking in depth references, you may learn that the guy or gal quoting your kitchen, was building decks or laying shingles three to five years ago. If he or she was honest with you, that shouldn't cost them the job. Everyone wants to improve themselves. However, it should raise a warning flag. You have to be extra sure he or she knows what they are doing and that they are very meticulous. When comparing quotes, make sure they know what they are talking about. Their error, could wind up costing you (not saving) thousands of dollars.

If they can not, or will not, give you the references you require, do not even consider the organization. A salesman who talks down the concept of references, saying things like, "You know I wouldn't tell you the name of anyone who wasn't going to say I was wonderful," can not be trusted. Get rid of him.

After you have checked the references and decided on the best quote, it is time for contract signing.

Living with a Contractor

The Modernization Contract

The modernization contract is the key ingredient to assuring that you will get a good job. The "standard contract" you are given to sign when the contractor asks for your down payment is usually loaded against you.

First of all, there is no "standard" modernization contract. If your contractor paid good money to have a "standard" form printed, you can be sure it has been fine tuned, and is loaded with paragraphs designed to protect the contractor, not you.

If a contractors association has put together a "standard contract", it often means that a bunch of really high priced lawyers got together to create a document that gives the contractor loads of weasel room and severely restricts the homeowner's rights.

The best way to protect your rights and assure a good, remodeling job is to insist that the following information is included in your contract. The contractor, or his sales representative, may say that there is no room for this information on their contract form. That's OK. You don't need a printed contract form.

Let the contractor retype the contract, putting in all the required information. Along the way, he will also have to put all the fine print designed to snare the unwary into legible type so that you can actually read what you are agreeing to. This will enable you to ask intelligent questions.

Living with a Contractor

If the contractor protests, make me the bad guy. Give him or her a photocopy of this portion of the chapter.

On the day of the signing use this section as a check off sheet. Don't sign until every point is covered. Don't let the contractor bully you. If the contractor refuses to put any of this information in your contract, he or she should not be given the job.

Information You Need in The Contract

1. Complete name of the modernization company.

2. Name of the head of company, the Qualifying Officer (the person who holds the builders license for the company), and the name of the production manager.

3. Address of company.

4. Statement that the company will obtain all necessary building permits and blue prints, and what the costs shall be for these items.

5. Listing of Company's Workmen's Compensation and Casualty Insurance Company names and policy numbers and a statement that you will receive certificates of insurance from the insurance companies or their agents before work begins.

6. Builder's License number of both the company and the qualifying officer.

Living with a Contractor

7. Exact description of the work to be done, including all dimensions.

8. Drawing of work to be done showing location of all doors, windows, stairways, or special features. In the event of a simple modernization, such as furnace replacement, this item can be eliminated.

9. Listing of all special materials or equipment to be used in the modernization. This listing must include the Manufacturer's name, trade and model name, model number, and exact dimensions. Never allow the term "industry standard" to be included in your contract. It will usually be used to short change you.

For example, if a door is being installed, list who makes it, what the name and model number of the exact door is, and the dimensions of the door. If it is an exterior door, also require the name, description, and model number of the lock set.

10. Clean up and trash pick up is part of the job. Make certain that the contract lists who will be responsible for what, when.

11. Statement that you will receive Full Unconditional Waivers stating that all construction lien rights to your property are being relinquished by the sub contractors, employees and/or building materials suppliers, before you are required to pay their bills.

Living with a Contractor

In other words, if concrete work is done, you pay for the concrete work after the concrete company and the subcontractor who actually did the concrete work, have been paid and supplied, signed, Full Unconditional Waiver of Lien Forms to the builder.

This is not too much to ask. Your down payment assures that the builder has the money to do this. The builder gives you the Full Unconditional Waiver Forms along with his invoice when he or she asks for payment.

"Full" and "Unconditional" are the two most important words. A Full Conditional, or a Partial Waiver means that you could still be on the hook.

This is one of the most critical parts of the entire agreement. In many States if you do not get Release of Lien forms signed by the materials suppliers and the subcontractors, they have a right to lien your property if they do not get paid by the builder. This means that even though you have already paid the builder in full, you could be forced to pay for the job twice in order to clear the title on your property.

12. Statement that you will receive copies of all product or equipment guarantees or warranties used in conjunction with the job after it is paid in full.

13. Statement that all work shall be done in compliance with, or exceeding, applicable State, City, and County Building Codes, and that all work will be inspected and approved by the appropriate inspectors.

Living with a Contractor

14. Guaranteed start and completion dates. The comple-
    tion date is most important. A penalty clause should
    be included, specifying money to be paid to you if
    the work is not completed by the completion date.
    Likewise a bonus extra payment should be specified
    that will be paid the builder if the work is done
    before completion date.

15. Itemization of how additional costs shall be deter-
    mined if unforeseen, but necessary, work is needed
    once the job has begun.

16. Payment terms. I don't care if the builder is your
    brother, never pay more than 30% down. Payments
    should always be linked to task completions and the
    receipt of Release of Lien Forms signed by the perti-
    nent subcontractors and building materials suppli-
    ers. Always hold back at least 10% until the job has
    been finished to your satisfaction, all cleanup has
    been completed, and all trash taken to dump.

This may sound like a lot of work, it is. Would you
rather do the work and be sure of what you are getting, or
not do the work and run the risk of getting into trouble
later? Play it smart. Get the information you need written
into your modernization contract. Then sit back and brag
about the results!

Living with a Contractor

How to Live with a Contractor

Believe it. Your contractor is far more important to your marriage, and can have a far greater impact on your life and your bank account, than your brother-in-law. Once the decision is made to modify your house, and you have turned a major job over to a builder, you do live with him or her for the duration of the project.

Your significant other is a piece of cake. You don't know what exasperation is until you walk in and see the new fireplace installed at the wrong end of a room, or a picture window that is too small; a wall that mysteriously goes on an angle, or a roof with shingles that look like they are part of a crazy quilt.

If you choose the wrong contractor, all of these things can happen. Even with the best contractor in the world, some trying moments will occur. The best thing for you is to know that some trying things are going to happen so be very businesslike about it.

Pat Murphy, a friend of mine who is considered by many to be one of the best building inspectors in the business, always tells people two things:

"Living through a major remodeling job is often the acid test of a marriage. If you can't live with extreme stress, don't remodel."

Living with a Contractor

and

"Expect a mess. No matter what they promise, the building trades never clean up after themselves."

There are three ways to maintain peace and tranquillity during a major modernization.

1. Arrange to be out of town and let some one else be responsible.

2. Establish ground rules early. Talk everything out with the production manager and make sure he knows your needs. He won't always be able to comply with them, but at least you'll have a common point of reference.

3. Give up and quiver in a corner until its over.

To you, your home is your place of refuge. To a builder, it is a work site. This gives you two very different points of view. Good builders try to relate, but it's hard.

Before construction (or destruction) starts, meet with the production manager. The production manager may be the builder or whomever he or she has delegated to be in charge of the day to day work on the job.

Spell out the ground rules for the job. If you have days they positively can't be on the job, tell him. If you

Living with a Contractor

have some delicate bushes or plants that can't be trampled, tell him. It may not do any good, but at least, you'll have told him. If it is vital, put it in writing in duplicate and have him sign a copy.

This is a good time to check your files and make certain that the builder's casualty and workmen's compensation insurance companies have sent you certificates of insurance. If they haven't, let the production manager know that no one will be allowed to work on your house until those certificates of insurance are in your possession.

This is critically important. If the builder does not have insurance, especially workman's compensation insurance, and a calamity happens, you could lose your house. While we're talking insurance, did you call your insurance agent and ask if you need some kind of a rider on your homeowners policy to give you extra protection during the period of construction?

Some states or municipalities demand that the builder posts a performance bond. It adds to the overall cost of the job but is a real benefit to you. If bonds are a requirement, have you received your copy?

Find out what time the workers should be on the site in the morning; when they usually take their breaks; when they usually quit for the day; when you should expect that the major deliveries will arrive and what they should contain.

Living with a Contractor

Once construction is underway, consider your house a place of business. Ladies dressed in thong bikinis may get a lot of admiring attention, but as a homeowner, you would rather that the workers keep their mind on their work rather than enjoy the view. Make sure that everyone in the family realizes that there is a dress code while your job is under construction.

Letting the construction crew know which rest room they can use and where they can get a plentiful supply of fresh water is nice. Providing a couple of cold six packs of pop and a friendly atmosphere will usually pay dividends. Never offer beer or any other alcoholic beverages. They are not permitted at Ford or General Motors. They don't belong on your work site either.

You want the work to be done as rapidly as possible. Usually that means that you should stay out of their way. Don't help unless specifically asked, or you have made a specific arrangement to work along side the crew.

Set up an accordion file on the job. Include all vital pieces of information including certificates of insurance, copies of the contract and any revisions, your copy of the blueprints, receipts for any materials you buy, all receipts you receive, mortgage or loan agreements, notice of furnishing, and release for lien forms.

Living with a Contractor

Keep a diary. Make a thorough, day by day record of who was doing what, when, on your job. Write down what deliveries were made and what was delivered. If you can, check out the deliveries to make certain that everything that is supposed to go into the job is actually being delivered.

Don't just write about things that happen, make entries on days when nothing happens. There may be perfectly good reasons for this inactivity; the carpenters may have to stop work until plumbers or electricians have accomplished something, or certain materials may be unavailable. What ever it is, you want to know about it and log it in your diary.

Keep a scratch pad with a piece of carbon paper. If you see something that is going wrong, or something that is in the wrong place, don't just tell the workmen. Put it in writing, sign it, date it, and make sure the building superintendent gets the note.

Your carbon copy should go into the accordion file under changes and corrections. It becomes a permanent record of the job. If something is going wrong or is not part of the approved plan, and you tried to stop it, you shouldn't have to pay for it. Your carbon copies can save you big money during the final reconciliation of the bill.

Living with a Contractor

If something critical is going wrong, call the builder about it. If it is not corrected immediately write a letter to the builder and send it certified mail, return receipt requested. Keep the receipt with your carbon or photo copy of the letter.

Keep a record of all inspections. Write down who inspected what, when. Be sure to put down the names and phone numbers of the building inspectors.

It is also a great idea to shoot pictures, or make a video during construction. Don't get in the way, but maintain a visual record of the carpenters, electricians, plumbers and what they are doing.

Hopefully you will just use those pictures when you brag about the job. Or, years from now, when someone needs to know how much insulation is behind "that" wall, you'll be able to whip out a photo and show them.

In the worse case scenario, and things go wrong, the photo and diary may serve as vital pieces of evidence allowing you to present a formidable case.

If an accident happens, be sure to make a record of it. Shoot pictures and include a complete description in your diary.

Living with a Contractor

When the job is done, the workmen will clean up after themselves. There will undoubtedly be some scrap lumber and other materials that they throw away.

There may also be some fresh lumber and materials left over. These materials are not scrap. They do not belong to you. They were not figured into the cost of your job. They are the builder's property. A good builder will often send out more materials than he needs on the job, so that if the carpenters or other workmen make mistakes, work can continue.

The materials will be picked up by the construction department and delivered to another job site. If the builder does not want to pick up the materials, he will ask you if you want them. Until then, they belong to him. It will penalize him unfairly and cut into his honest profit if those materials disappear. Please do not make yourself look bad by trying to keep something that does not belong to you.

One more thing. Once the job is completed and you know you've found a great contractor, brag about him or her. Tell all your friends and neighbors. Good people are hard to find.

By bragging about your contractor, you increase his or her business and become a more valuable customer.

Living with a Contractor

How to Fire a Bad Contractor

Living with a Contractor

How to Fire a Bad Contractor

If you hired your builder properly, this section should not apply to you. Every once in a long while, even the best of builders has a job that goes wrong. It may not have anything to do with the job.

A crew chief, who has been the builder's best man for the past ten years, may be getting a divorce and not give a darn who shows up or where he is pounding nails.

The last three jobs may have been under quoted by a salesman, and the builder may be suffering a temporary cash flow problem.

The production manager may get sick and be out for weeks.

In the best of all possible worlds, none of these things would have any effect on your job. In the real world, they do. In the worst case scenario, major portions of your job may have to be rebuilt, or the job may be, at least temporarily, abandoned. I have seen jobs that were left unfinished for almost a year.

When the job goes bad, you may be forced, regretfully, either to stop construction, continue construction with another builder, or complete construction by sub contracting out the remainder of the job yourself.

Living with a Contractor

First word of advice: Do not be hasty. Do everything possible to get the work completed by the original builder. If you decide that will not work, take no action until you have talked with your family attorney. Even he may want you to consult an attorney who is an expert in your State's building laws before you do anything.

Long before the job becomes a crisis, you should make telephone calls, then write a certified letter to the builder outlining the problem and giving him fifteen days to respond.

If there is no response during that fifteen day period, contact your attorney and follow his advice.

In some circumstances, let's say the builder's crew left your roof open, and won't come back even though rain is pouring in, damaging your house, you can take immediate action to correct the problem and pass the costs on to the builder.

However, in most circumstances, if the builder has a valid contract with you and there are no time conditions for completion or termination, you may be required to pay the builder for the entire contract, even if you or another builder you hired, completed the majority of the work.

I am not an attorney (I have a hard enough time being a good talk show host), but here are the steps I recommend you take if you sense your job is going bad.

Living with a Contractor

What You Should Do If the Job Goes Bad.

1. Make every effort to complete the job without litigation.

2. Put the complaints in writing. Give a definite time period for the work to be completed.

3. Meet with the builder personally, and bring along a friend who can be called as a witness. Go over the job, listing your complaints, and get the builder's solution.

4. Find out what the real reasons are for the problems. Are workers unpaid? Aren't there enough materials to complete the job due to a cash flow problem? Has the builder sold too many jobs to finish yours in a timely manner?

5. Contact the building inspector, report the problem, ask his advice and see if he will call the builder.

6. Analyze your contract. See what work has been done, versus what work has been paid for. How many payments may you still be obligated to pay?

What is the status of the materials left on the site. Do you own them? Are they paid for? Can you use them without accepting undue liability? Should you have the materials picked up by the building materials dealer if they have been left on your site for a long period of time?

Living with a Contractor

7. If your State or County has a policing body delegated with the responsibility of enforcing building contracts, make out a formal complaint.

8. If all the above has not gotten you satisfactory results, consult your lawyer and start taking formal legal steps to either have the job completed by the builder, or the contract terminated so that the work can be reassigned to another builder.

9. After your attorney (not you), has taken the steps necessary to terminate the contract for non-performance, you may safely have the work completed by another builder.

Sorry if I frightened you. These bad things will not happen on your job. But, just on the off chance that you turn out to be that one in a million, it's a good idea to know all the possibilities.

Chapter 3
How Long Should It Take?

How Long Should It Take?

A Builder's Perspective

OK, now that we know how to hire a contractor, how long should the job take?

To get a builder's perspective, I asked Adam Helfman. Adam represents the fourth generation at his family's firm, Fairway Construction. His grandfather held the patent for dormers (second story additions). Fairway Construction is consistently rated among the top fifty remodelers in the country and has been rated #1 Regionally and Nationally by the National Association of the Remodeling Industry (NARI).

If the folks at Fairway don't know how long a job should take, nobody does.

Here's Adam's estimate, of the time it takes for a major remodeling job, like a big kitchen or room addition, to be sold, designed, processed, and built, listed as a spread sheet.

Step by Step

Adam Helfman was very quick to point out that every job is different. Building a small deck or installing windows, or re-roofing a house can be accomplished in just a few days after the permits are pulled and construction starts.

How Long Should It Take?

Major Remodeling Time Frame		
Task	**Number Minimum**	**Days Maximum**
Sit down meeting with salesman/designer	1	1
Days to final plan	7	14
Blue Prints from architect	7	28
Request for Building Permit	14	30
Changes to Conform to Code	0	60
Hand Off Meeting	1	7
Special Orders	28	42
Time to start date	35	56
Actual Construction	14	35
Total Days	**107**	**273**

The First Important Date

The first important date from the contractor's point of view is when you and your significant other sit down with the company's representative.

In a larger company it may be a salesman or a designer. In a smaller firm, it may be the contractor. Whoever it is, it's called a "Sit down" in the trade and it represents Day 1 on your time line.

How Long Should It Take?

It is really important that, if there is someone else who will have significant impact on the final decision, both of you be at this first meeting. Don't play games or think your time is too valuable.

Why You Both Need To Be There

If one of you comes in later and has significant input into the planning and final design specifications, it can result in the builder's time line being turned all the way back to Day 1. Remember, you may be the customer, but in today's economy, a designer's time is very valuable. Invariably, the best work is done for the people who are best organized and approach their remodeling job with an open, business like attitude.

Delays and backtracking result in exasperation for the builder, as well as family arguments, wasted time, and higher prices, for you. And, heaven forbid, if they have actually started hammering when the changes are made.

Then it becomes like a government job: perfectly good lumber becomes scrap; pipe is thrown away; time estimates and costs go out of sight; and the miffed home-owner, complains: "All I did was move the sink from there to there."

If all goes well that first night, the builder or designer may be able to make a rough sketch or listing of what you want and make some preliminary measure-

How Long Should It Take?

ments. There is a good possibility that some of your desires may have to be rethought right then, because what you want may not be practical or affordable.

The representative will schedule another appointment for a week to ten days in the future. During the interval, a work request will make its way through the planning department. Someone may be sent out to the house to make some more measurements. Preliminary financing work may be started.

Decision Time

On the second, third, or fourth meeting, a final plan and a cost estimate will be submitted and agreed to. By this time you will have made the decision to go with the genuine cherry wood cabinets instead of the eurostyle cabinetry that first caught your eye. You may have specified Delta faucets and Merillat cabinets, or Andersen or Pella windows. This entire procedure usually takes two to four weeks. We say 7 to 14 days on the spread sheet.

After the final plan and terms have been agreed to, and the contract signed, the job will go to the architect to have blueprints drawn so a final materials list can be drawn up and necessary permits applied for. The blueprints are then submitted to the homeowner for approval. Drawing of blueprints from an approved plan and print approval by the homeowner is usually accomplished in a week.

How Long Should It Take?

Who's House Is This Anyway?
Permits & Building Department Approval

You just think it's your house because they let you pay the mortgage and property taxes. In almost every political subdivision in the United States, the builder has to apply for permits from your city or municipality, Home Owners Association, pay necessary fees, and post required bonds. The Building Department checks the plans for Building Code or Zone violations.

Building Department approval and the awarding of permits generally takes from two weeks to a month. If there is a great deal of building going on in your area and building inspectors are stretched to the limit, it may take a great deal longer to get a permit. Some major cities are so incompetent that it may take three to six months for permit approval.

Violations & Appeals

The Building Department may find that your plans are in violation of the City or Municipality's building or zone codes. If your plans are in violation the plans either have to be changed, or you may be required to go before an appeals board for a "variance," permission to build or modify a structure that in not in compliance with code.

How Long Should It Take?

From a time stand point, it is usually better to modify your plans to conform to code, rather than making an appeal. Appeals take time, which translates into money and frustration. Besides, if you make an appeal, there is no assurance that your appeal will be granted. If you have to go through this procedure it can add up to two months to your building process.

The Hand Off Meeting

Once permits are received, many builders like to have what is called a "hand off" meeting. The builder or his representative, the designer, and the job superintendent, meets with both homeowners and the job is formally handed over from the planning department to the building department.

This is a very important meeting because it is the homeowners last chance to make changes to the plans while they are still just lines on paper.

It is also an opportunity for you to meet the man or woman who will actually be responsible for building your job. You get to size him or her up, to assure yourself that he or she is the type of person you have confidence in.

How Long Should It Take?

You also get to point out specifics you want to make certain the building superintendent understands. This includes important things like, "that built in china cabinet has to be lighted to show off my crystal collection;" or "The commode being built into the room addition has to be very quiet because I will be having business meetings in the adjoining room."

Since everything is very "palsy-walsy" during this meeting, it is usually a good time to look at the building superintendent like you wanted him to marry your daughter and inherit the majority of your estate, then get him to give you his beeper, car and home phone numbers. You may wish you had them later.

Setting up the "hand off" meeting can take anywhere from a day to a week, depending on your, and the builder's, time schedules.

Special Orders

After the meeting, the building department sends out for any special orders that are necessary to complete your job. Special Orders are usually cabinets, hardware, plumbing or electrical, special tiles, wood, windows or doors.

The special ordering and receiving process usually takes four to six weeks. If you want something that is very exotic, or in extremely short supply, it can take months.

How Long Should It Take?

Exotic items may cause for a special consultation between homeowner and builders representatives. Just what do you want to do if the items are not readily available?

The temptation is to start the job without all the items being there. This is usually a bad move because once the job starts, your home will be in a partially "torn up" condition, until the last special order has been installed.

Trying to entertain with wiring hanging out of the walls where an errant fixture will one day be placed is enough to make a person wince. Trying to cook a meal without countertops is more than enough to make you want to tear your hair.

Start Date

When all the special orders are in, your job can be scheduled for construction and a "start date" assigned. That means your job gets to stand in line waiting for an available crew. If you have a popular, and well organized builder, he or she is completely scheduled at least eight to ten weeks ahead. A start date is not cast in stone. Mother Nature may decide to take a hand. Emergencies come up. Prior jobs take longer than planned.

How Long Should It Take?

Construction

Once actual construction begins, the work should be completed in two to five weeks depending on the complexity of the job, the availability of crews, and the speed with which building inspectors give approval to the various stages of construction.

In some parts of the country building tradesmen are in very short supply. Sometimes jobs are held up for weeks waiting for a plumber, electrician, stone mason, wood floor installer, etc., to find time to complete his part of the job.

On the average job, building inspectors may have to be on site five times or more: foundations, rough construction, electrical, plumbing, and final construction. If anything doesn't pass, the job can be held up for days waiting for reconstruction and re-inspection.

Where Is Everybody?

During the construction phase you may find that the trades just mysteriously stop work and disappear. This sort of surprise shouldn't happen if you and the building superintendent are in regular communication.

When it does, it usually means that work has stopped for an inspection that is required to be made

How Long Should It Take?

before work can continue or that work has stopped to allow plumbers, electricians, or other specialists to do their work.

It can also be a warning signal that the contractor isn't paying his crews and they have just stopped work; that the supervisor isn't doing his job; or that necessary materials aren't arriving. If you have not been forewarned about the work stoppage, it's time to get out the superintendent's beeper, car and home phone numbers and find out why.

After reading all this, you may think that you could build a house in the time it takes to construct a major renovation. You could. In fact, you might be able to build a house quicker. Most of the same permits are needed. The same trades are required. There are few, if any, special orders. New construction often has a higher priority on the building inspector's "To Do" list.

Total Time

You can estimate that the total amount of time needed for a major renovation, from your initial appointment to final completion, is 107 to 273 days. That translates to four and a half to seven months. Very little of that time should actually be upsetting your house.

How Long Should It Take?

Most of it is office work you never see, or logistics you never think about. After you select a good builder, try hard to work with him, meet his time requirements, and you may be pleasantly surprised at the time you will save.

Section II
Living Space

The Chapters in this Section are devoted to expanding and revitalizing the areas in which we live.

The kitchen and bath are the two most important and expensive rooms in the house, so they get their own chapters.

Room additions come next. Then we go downstairs to solve the special challenges of converting the basement into living space.

Chapter 4
Kitchens

Kitchens

Upgrading the Kitchen

I'm often asked if it is worth the money to remodel a kitchen or bath if a person is just going to live in a house a few more years. I believe, that if the work is well done, it is a win - win situation for everyone. You get to enjoy the new kitchen or bath while you're there, and when it comes time to sell, you have a much more salable house.

The kitchen and bath are the two most important rooms in your house. After prospective buyers have looked at your home's exterior, including the all important roof line, and decided they like what they see, the next things they look at are the kitchen and bath.

More than any others, these two rooms are usually the deciding factors on whether prospective buyers want to move in or move on. Anything you do to upgrade these areas increases the salability of the house.

On a square foot basis, the kitchen and bath are the two most expensive rooms of the house. More fixtures and appliances are concentrated in these areas than anywhere else.

The kitchen and bath are the center of a house. The heart is the kitchen. The bath, especially the master bath, can make or break a sale. What you do in these rooms is extremely important.

Kitchens

Cost Vs Value Study

Every year, *Remodeling* Magazine publishes an exclusive Cost Vs Value report[1] which tells the ROI (Return on Investment) a remodeling buyer could expect if he or she sold the house within twelve months of having the project done.

In the 96/97 study Kitchens and Baths led the way. It was projected that a minor kitchen remodel would repay 94% of the investment if the house was sold within one year. A bathroom addition returned 91%. A Major kitchen remodel returned 90% and a bathroom remodel returned 77%.

None of these figures allow for the increased salability of the house after the remodeling project was completed.

Kitchens and baths are often spoken, written and merchandised together. This is much as it should be. Both use cabinets. Both need hot and cold running water. One way or the other, both are concerned with food processing.

Despite their similarities, they are two very different rooms. For the rest of this chapter, we're going to concentrate on kitchens. The next chapter will focus on baths.

---

[1] Remodeling Magazine, October 1996, Cost Vs Value Survey, p 67-82; Hanley-Wood, Inc., One Thomas Circle NW #600, Washington, DC 20005. For more information call 202-736-3444.

Kitchens

Almost everyone has heard (horror) stories about someone's $30, $40, or $50,000 kitchen renovation. However, Kitchen & Bath Business (KBB) did a survey of 20,000 consumers and discovered that 77% of the people who remodeled their kitchens spent less than $10,000. Forty-nine percent spent under $5,000.

You can spend as much or as little as you want. A couple of gallons of paint and a little creativity with borders and shelving can give a completely new look.

The most important things you can do while still in the dreaming stage is to study and plan. Go to the library and book stores. Look at magazines. Photocopy pertinent pages and start creating a file.

Call the National Kitchen & Bath Association and ask them for their free Kitchen and Bath Planning Kit.[2] The kit contains a useful brochure on kitchen and bath planning, the names and addresses of nearby National Kitchen and Bath Association members, national manufacturers, and a pad of square ruled paper, all for Glenn Haege's favorite price: Free.

---

[2] See Supplier's Phone List in Appendix..

Kitchens

Planning a Kitchen

Measure and draw both a horizontal and a vertical diagram of your kitchen. Start from one corner of the room and show specific measurements to the windows, doors, sink, etc. Show all measurements in inches. You measure in inches because cabinets are measured in inches. Be certain to put down exact measurements. If it is 54 1/4", write down 54 1/4". That extra 1/4" might be all it takes for a length of cabinets to fit.

Measure doors and windows from the outer edge of the door frame to the outer edge of the door frame. This may mean that you will measure 36" for a 30" wide door. Show whether doors swing in or out.

Measure the distances to all electric, gas and water outlets.

Do a vertical drawing. Show total height, distance windows are from floor, height of window (outer edge of frame to outer edge of frame), distance from window frame to ceiling. Make the same measurements for all doors. Also show the distance of floor to gas and water pipes and electrical outlets. Do detail drawings if necessary.

Kitchens

Cross check your measurements by adding up all the pertinent detail measurements and seeing if they add up to the width or length of the room.

Now you know what reality is. You can look at the present outline of your room, and decide how you would like to rearrange spaces. When you go to talk to kitchen designers, take the room diagrams with you.

Make some to scale cut-outs of the appliances, cabinets, tables, chairs, etc.. Play around with different groupings. Discuss them. Get some square ruled paper and lay out your ideas. This is your "writer's rough." It will be, should be, changed countless times before your dream becomes a reality.

Go to kitchen and bath centers. Learn the names of your area's leading distributors and visit their showrooms. Talk to people. Ask about prices. Pick up brochures. Decide what gives the most bang for the buck for you, your family, your life-style.

Here are some basic appliance widths to include in your plan: Refrigerator: 36" wide; Sinks: Double-Bowl: 36", Single-Bowl: 27"; Dishwasher: 24"; Built-in Wall Oven: 30"; Microwave: 24"; Free Standing Range: 30" (older ranges, and some of the most expensive new ones can go up to 42" or more); Built-in Cook top: 36". Cabinets come in various lengths.

Kitchens

If you are a computer whiz, go to your local computer store or consult the computer catalogs. There are some very good kitchen planning guides out there. If you can find the some at the computer store, get permission to check out the program before you buy. Make sure the program works with you, not against you. If you find one you like, its the perfect way to plan a kitchen, because the computer does the math, makes sure that everything fits, and gives you very realistic reproductions of what your kitchen will look like when it is complete.

When you've got your rough plan completed, and have collected most of your pictures, take your ideas and start in-depth discussions with the pros at kitchen and bath centers. Looking at your plans, the really good designers will suggest some great ways to enhance your ideas and make them even better. Listen to them.

It makes good sense to pay for talent. A designer doesn't work for free. So if you are going to have a plan worked up, then quoted by several different companies, pay for the design up front. That way you can feel free to show the design to as many people as you want and there will be no hard feelings if the first designer's company does not get the job.

Kitchens

Kitchen Features

The kitchen is a lot more than just a food preparation area. It is the heart of the home. Before you renovate, list all the things you do there. Are you happy with the current lay out of the kitchen? What could be done to make the kitchen more efficient? If the kitchen is at least 10' X 12', could the floor plan be redesigned to include an island? Are you making maximum use of the room you have?

In my house, family and friends tend to congregate in the kitchen. We may spend the majority of the evening there. I spoke to the Director of one of the nation's largest building associations recently. He is a man with more sophistication, money, and a larger house than I will ever have. His friends cluster in the kitchen, too.

If the same is true with your family, decide whether you want your kitchen renovation to reflect this entertainment function. If so, consider more seating, conversation nooks, maybe even a fireplace.

How about a small desk or computer area? Some women have all their recipes, the family budget, household security, all running from their kitchen command post. Does this sound like you?

Kitchens

If not, perhaps you are a person that would enjoy converting this space to a display area for your cook book collection, or kitchen collectibles, that would reflect your personality and bring a smile to your face every time you enter the room.

Kathy, my editor, discovered that coffee mugs she gathered over the years, reflected every major milestone of her life: school, university, post graduate degrees, marriage, baby, career growth and changes. That collection of coffee mugs, showcased in her kitchen, is a great conversation starter and makes the kitchen uniquely hers. What would tell the world about you?

What Should Be Replaced?

Everything. It really depends upon the present condition of your kitchen. If it is too dark, consider new windows, garden windows, sky lights, and improved lighting. The new tubular skylights can make a vast difference in the amount of natural light you have in your kitchen.

There is also a vast array of lighting fixtures available today. Everything from track lighting to miniatures that easily fit inside, above or under cabinets. Eliminate the dark spots and you will enjoy your kitchen more.

Kitchens

Most older kitchens do not have enough electric power for today's modern kitchen needs. Make sure you have at least 150 amp service and several dedicated kitchen circuits. Consider dedicated lines to counter top areas where you run your major appliances. Remember, unless you like resetting the circuits every time you make a piece of toast, listen to the radio or TV, and use the microwave at the same time, each major appliance deserves its own circuit.

If the cabinets are old and not works of art, replace or reface. How about glassed in cabinet doors that would not only show off your dishes, but would make it easy for anyone to put them away after washing? Naturally, pots and pans deserve their own hanging display. How about a wine rack? Don't you really deserve a broom closet?

Consider using top-of-the-line tile treatments. Hand painted and mosaic tiles and tile murals are becoming very popular in both the kitchen and bath.

Be sure to include features that make it easy to access every area, and store equipment and supplies efficiently.

Kitchens

Do not be put off by the high price of custom cabinets. Many manufacturers have now come out with lower priced stock cabinet lines that look as good, and wear as well, as the custom variety. You have to look and not let yourself be limited by one retailer's, or one remodeler's, product lines and prices.

I've included names, phone numbers, and even some internet addresses of a number of cabinet makers in the Appendix at the back of the book. Call some of them direct. Ask for brochures and price lists. Find out who stocks them in your area.

Paint and wallpaper are very important. Wallpaper borders or stencils can give a kitchen a delightful personality. Faux finishes make the room uniquely your own.

If you would like to try a faux finish, but are afraid to attempt it, get a copy of my book, *TAKE THE PAIN OUT OF PAINTING -INTERIORS-*, it has a 40 page faux finishing section that takes you by the hand and gives you step by step instructions on how to stencil, and use techniques like sponging, rag rolling, feather dusting, combing, etc.

Also consider upgrading countertops, sinks, faucets, garbage disposals, floors and appliances. DuPont Corian and other newly developed composite materials make highly attractive countertops that will not stain or scratch. Wilsonart's Solid-Surface Veneer gives you most of the properties of a solid surface at a lower installed price.

Kitchens

Sinks now come in a wide selection of materials, not just porcelain and stainless steel.

Top of the line appliances can sell a house. Many an upwardly mobile, two career couple has bought a house because they lusted after the gleaming, stainless steel, professional stove. Even if they have all their parties catered, in their mind's eyes, they saw themselves making breads, pastries and roasts in the huge convection ovens. These are the things that dreams are made of.

One caveat, before I convince you to invest your life savings in your kitchen: the value and features of your house should stay in proportion to your neighborhood.

If you live in a hot residential area, and your neighbors are investing in paver walks and deluxe shadow line shingles, feel free to make your home the best it can be. If real estate values are almost stagnant, upgrading is an investment in your home, not your house. What you do is for you. To maximize on your investment, renovate, but keep it practical.

Remember, not everything has to be done at one time. If you have a master plan, do the basics now, and you can upgrade the appliances later.

Kitchens

The Best Way to Get a Good Deal on Kitchen Cabinets

Shop 'til you drop is no misnomer when it comes to cabinets. Cabinets are always expensive. But the price for the same cabinet, or same quality cabinet, may vary greatly from retailer to retailer, or contractor to contractor.

There are a few large manufacturers, like Merillat, then literally thousands of variously sized manufacturers from the United States and Europe.

Some of the mom and pop's build cabinetry of the very highest quality. Their volume is so low that they can afford to pick and choose wood very carefully. Others staple together cabinets of cheap materials and, while they may look good for initial installation, they have no lasting quality.

If your renovation is being done by a contractor, you must rely on him. However, part of your selection process should have been checking him or her out. That means not only looking at finished jobs, but asking about their cabinets. Why does the contractor offer this particular brand? What is its track record? Check out jobs that are a few years old. How are the cabinets holding up. Do they still look like quality?

Kitchens

Can I Install the Cabinets Myself and Save Some Money?

Installing cabinets is like installing windows. A simple thing like measuring cabinets is an art. If you have the skills of a finish carpenter, you can save a good deal of money. If you aren't and want a professional looking job, hire the best talent you can find.

My Kitchen Cabinets Are Stained Dark, I Want to Paint Them a Light Color. Can I Refinish, or Do I Have to Replace?

If you wanted to remove all the color and dark stain, then re-stain a lighter color, I would say it's not worth the trouble. Get new cabinets. Since you just want to paint the cabinets, we are okay.

Materials needed: 80 or 100 Grit Sand Paper, Ammonia Based Wax Stripper for Vinyl Floors, like New Beginnings by Armstrong, Oil Based Stain Kill like Cover Stain, or Kilz, and Oil Base Enamel Paint.

Equipment needed: Buckets, Paper Drop Clothes, Rubber Gloves, 2 Sponges, 2 1/2" China Bristle Brush, Paint Buckets.

1. First we want to take all those lumps and the bumps out. Use a 100 grit or 80 grit. Sand the lumps and

bumps down. Most cabinets just have to be powder sanded to provide a good profile for the new paint.

2. Lay paper or cloth drop cloths. Protect everything that you are not going to clean because you do not want any cleaner to come in contact with counter tops, floors, appliances or plants. Plastic drop cloths get too slippery. Use paper, canvas, a bed sheet, something that yet still provides a non-slip foundation.

3. Remove the doors from the cabinets, and clean them separately. Be sure to remove all the hardware from the doors before cleaning.

4. Remove the hinges on the cabinets.

5. Clean the inside and outside of the cabinets. Wash them with a 2 bucket process. One bucket contains the ammonia based wax stripper for vinyl floors, the other clear rinse water. One of the brand names on the market is "New Beginnings" by Armstrong, but most cleaning product manufacturers make an ammonia based wax stripper.

Make sure you buy a stripper, not a cleaner/stripper. The wax stripper has a lot of ammonia. Ammonia and varnish hate each other. In this case that is good. The ammonia will chemically burn a profile into the kitchen cabinets.

Kitchens

Wear goggles and fold cuffs on your rubber gloves so that none of the solution drains down your forearms.

Mix up the solution according to label solution, about 4 to 6 oz. of stripper per gallon, in one bucket. Fill the other bucket with rinse water. Use two sponges. One for the stripper, the other for the rinse water.

Put on the solution liberally. You do not have to scrub. Let it sit for a couple of minutes, then rinse twice. The cleaner does the work and not the grease in your elbow. Throw the rinse water away every three cabinets.

6. After the cabinets are rinsed, let them dry one day.

7. Apply an oil based stain kill. The product may not say oil based stain kill on the label. Quite often the term used is "stain killer". One brand names is Cover Stain. Another is Kilz. Using an oil based stain killer is the secret to your success. The stain kill clamps the painted surface on to the cabinets and gives scuff and chip resistance.

Don't start screaming if the cabinet and door surfaces start looking blurry and blotchy. That is what it is supposed to look like. It is not a finish coat. It is a sealer.

Kitchens

Be sure to paint the inside of the kitchen cabinet. An inexpensive Whizz roller will make it easier for you to paint the back area.

8. Wait three to four hours for the stain kill to dry.

9. Apply the top coat. This is a very important room of your house, so splurge and select a top of the line oil base enamel semi-gloss for the top coat of the cabinets. You are going to pay a lot of money for this paint. It is going to be like a rock when it is done. Use a 2 1/2 inch china bristle brush.

Remember, paint cans are only for carrying and storing paint. When it comes time to use the paint, pour it into an inexpensive 1/2 gallon painting bucket that you can get at any paint store, hardware or home center

Dip the brush in the pail and then put the paint on with the brush. To smooth out all the stroke marks, the last strokes of the brush should be with the tips of the bristles. We call it tipping. Gently pull the brush down with just the tips of the bristles kissing the painted surface.

If you want to put another coat on, you have to do it within 36 hours. If you wait longer than 36 hours it will encourage inner coat peeling and chipping.

Kitchens

Replace or Reface?

If you love your present cabinets and just want to update them you may save 30 to 40% by refacing. If the cabinets are 20 - 30 years old, have been painted or stained half a dozen times, and are wearing out and just plain "yucky", replace.

If you really shop around you will be amazed at how close replacement cost can come to refacing.

One word of caution, always replace like with like or better. Do not let short term finances make the final decision. Cheaply made cabinets can look worn out after just a few years and will definitely be a liability when it comes time to sell your house. Fine craftsmanship in both manufacture and installation is also a key. The best cabinets, poorly installed are a disaster.

Inspect half a dozen of the kitchen jobs the contractor has done before giving him the contract. Make sure he or she used the finest finish carpenters for kitchen work.

What about the Counters?

Kitchen counter tops take a continual beating so neutral colors and reparable materials are very popular. Corian, Gibraltar, Surell, or Avonite.

Kitchens

If you like the solid surface look, but your budget says, "no way," at least spring for a large Corian, or other solid surface, cutting board. Solid surface edges can also create the solid surface counter look at a far lower cost.

Should I Put in a New Countertop Before or After Painting?

Do it before. Any kind of wood construction has to be done first and do the painting last.

What about Sinks?

You can spend as much or as little on sinks as your budget permits. Stainless steel used to be the sink of choice. Now, below level, solid surface sinks are taking the lead if your pocket book allows. Below level means they are mounted below the counter top to make clean up easier. Solid surfaces like Corian creates a sink that will stay attractive a long, long time.

If you are in the league that considers granite or poured concrete for countertops, you might also consider a tile front porcelain sink. They are beautiful, but very pricey. I am going to try very hard to make sure that my wife, Barbara never even sees one of these babies at any of the model homes we visit.

Kitchens

Do I Need a Water Filter?

Water filters are becoming the rage. Water for drinking and cooking should be the best tasting water of all. Point of Use (POU) filters that can be located right under the sink are increasingly popular.

When water filter shopping, low maintenance and constant water quality are the key elements. Lead and charcoal contact filters are the most popular in restaurant use so they might make the most noticeable difference in your use.

There is no room here, but I will include an in-depth overview of the selection and use of water filters in my next book, *Fix It Fast & Easy 3, Frantic Fixes.*

I Am Going to Change My Appliances at the Same Time I renovate the Kitchen. What is Your Opinion on Built-Ins?

Built-in appliances are beautiful and give a very custom look. They also cost twice as much as a stand alone appliance. In other words, a cook top costs as much as a free standing range, and a built-in oven costs as much as a range. On top of that you have to pay for the carpentry.

Kitchens

If money is a consideration, I suggest buying free standing appliances. You might also consider investing the extra money in really top of the line American, European, or professional appliances. They will give you a lot of bang for your buck.

I Want to Paint My Refrigerator. Can I Use the Same Oil Based Paint I Used on the Walls and Cabinets?

If this were a stove I would say, "Don't paint." If you want to replace all your appliances it is a waste of time. Since you only want to do a refrigerator and will not get the extreme heat stresses of a gas or electric stove, you can paint very successfully. I would recommend products that are a little bit harder, and more industrial oriented than ordinary paints. Look for words like high scrubability and heavy duty on the label.

Materials needed: 280 Grit Wet or Dry Sand Paper, Household Ammonia, Water base Stain Kill like Total One or Zinsser Bullseye 1-2-3, Very Tough Oil Base Enamel, Paint Sealant by Diamond Brite.

Equipment needed: Palm Sander, Rubber Gloves, Goggles, Sponge, Pail, China Bristle Brush.

Kitchens

1. Lightly sand the entire surface with 280 Grit Wet or Dry Sandpaper. You are not trying to take the paint off, just establish a profile. Using a palm sander is easiest.

2. Wash the refrigerator down with a solution of 4 oz. of ammonia to 2 quarts of water.

3. Rinse with water. Make it really squeaky clean.

4. Let dry thoroughly, wait at least 1 1/2 to 2 hours.

5. Apply a water base stain kill like Total One by Master Chem Industries.

6. Apply two coats of a very durable oil base enamel like Rustoleum. Use a china bristle brush.

The paint will dry rapidly, and you can use the refrigerator in six to twelve hours, but it takes seven days for water base stain kill to cure. Until then, you will be able to remove the paint with your fingernail. So be sure to wait seven days before washing or polishing it.

7. After seven days, apply a product called Paint Sealant by Diamond Brite. Diamond Brite seals and glazes the surface of the refrigerator. There are no cutters in it.

Kitchens

Be careful to buy the right product. If you buy a car wax, not a sealant, by mistake, it will cut the paint and come off on the rag you are using to polish the refrigerator. Put the Paint Sealant on all over the refrigerator. It will form a haze that you can buff into a beautiful, long lasting finish that is very easy to care for.

Are There Any Special Problems with Kitchen Floors?

The combination of water and heavy appliances means there is a good chance that you may have rotten, uneven flooring that has to be replaced. If this is the case, the original flooring has to be removed and the underlayment (the thin sheathing immediately below the flooring) or sub floor (usually 3/4" thick) repaired or replaced.

If the original flooring is perfectly flat and the only thing wrong with it is that it is old and worn, or just plain boring, you do not have to remove it, just put down a Luan underlayment on top of the old floor. It is relatively easy to re-cut doors to provide the necessary clearance at the bottom. However, if the addition of new flooring and Luan would make it difficult to access appliances for repair or replacement, it is best to remove the old flooring.

Kitchens

Can I Have a Hardwood Floor in the Kitchen?

Hardwood floors are becoming very popular in kitchens. If the existing floor is in fairly good shape, you can just lay the new wood flooring over the original.

Quite often wood floors in kitchens are called a "floating" floors. That means that the flooring is anchored to itself not the underlayment. It makes it easier for the floor to be laid on a less than perfect underlayment and helps protect the floor from water damage.

Most of the major wood flooring companies, like Hartco and Bruce, have prefinished wood flooring that is ideal for kitchen floor replacement. Hartco's Pattern Plus prefinished flooring is only 3/8" thick. Bruce Hardwood's Natural Reflections is only 5/16".

What about Vinyl Flooring?

Most kitchens floors are vinyl. Some of the new, high quality vinyls, like Mannigton Gold, have very specific installation requirements. They have to be installed by a certified installer. If you want the look of hardwood without the worry of water stains, there are now vinyl flooring styles which look just like hardwood.

Kitchens

Can I Install the Vinyl Flooring by Myself?

You can, but it is a lot easier if you let a professional install it. Some of the vinyls, like Mannington Gold, void the Warranty, if their product is not installed by a professional certified by them.

This is not just a whim. Many of the new products have very high gloss rates that will magnify any imperfection. Others telegraph the surface contours of the under layment. If the vinyl floor cover is not installed to precise directions, you will not be happy.

Kitchens

Chapter 5
Baths

Baths

Upgrading the Bath

One of the major plumbing manufacturer's research determined that the average bathroom is totally remodeled every thirty years. That isn't surprising. Almost nothing dates a house quicker than the bathroom.

Old bathrooms can be quaint, but usually they are just frustrating. You go into a bathroom for a definite purpose. You want the toilet quiet and functional. You want the sink attractive. You want the shower sanitary and invigorating. You want the tub relaxing. You want the total room to be clean, bright, and pleasing to the eye. That is quite a lot of "wants" to be serviced in the smallest room in the house.

While you will get a pay back for everything you do to upgrade the bath there is often not a need to replace the bathtub unless you have had major damage or are replacing it with a whirlpool. The tiles are usually OK, unless they've been cracked, you are removing the tub, or you just can't stand the antiquated style.

Your present toilet is often better than the one you would replace it with. If you must replace the commode, you can legally replace an existing 3 1/2 gallon reservoir commode with another one of the same size. Try finding a dealer who has a supply of the old commodes, or has set up a side line reconditioning old ones. This is definitely a case where old is better than new.

Baths

If you must replace the commode with a 1 1/2 gallon reservoir model to keep it color coordinated with the sink, etc., go top of the line. Many of the new commodes do not do the job adequately.

Baths are becoming leisure areas. Even though you cannot expand the floor space, there is a great deal you can do to upgrade it. One of the most popular items is a whirlpool bath. Improvements in design have made it possible to replace a standard tub with a same-size whirlpool model.

New, improved lighting is a must. A new mirror may be a necessity. Other noticeable improvements include DuPont Corian, or other composite material, countertops, sinks, and shower surround. You can also upgrade faucets, toilets and floors.

I don't have to tell you how hard those one inch by one inch floor tiles are to keep clean. If you have them, consider replacing them with larger floor tiles if possible.

Consider upgrading the ventilation. Some of the new ceiling exhaust fans are quieter and much more powerful than earlier models.

If you don't have a ceiling fan, install one. You will find that improving ventilation greatly reduces mildew and mold growth.

Baths

Is There Anything We Can Do to Make Our Small Bathroom Seem Larger?

Interior decorators tell me that you can fool people by using a lot of mirrors, maybe even an entire wall. If the bath is on the exterior wall side of the house, and you have got the budget, you can also install a bay or bow window. This could give you a good deal more space, extra counter top or seating area, plus a bright airy view.

Other tricks include installing waist high chair moldings, and laying the floor tile on an angle so that it accents the longest dimension of the room.

On the practical side, you should consider all the room between the studs as storage space just waiting to happen. On non-bearing walls you can cut several of the studs, and frame in recessed shelves or cabinets. Also consider a pedestal sink, or installing the vanity kitty-corner, so that it takes up less space.

Baths

Commodes

I started getting complaints as soon as the Environmental Protection Agency mandated 1.6 gallon toilets as the law of the land for new construction. The complaints go so bad that I played Sancho Panza to Rep. Joe Knollenberg's Don Quixote-like efforts to get the legislation reversed. We did manage to blanket Washington with a blizzard of toilet tissue proclaiming "Get the government out of my toilet," but were not successful in getting the necessary movement out of the bowels of Congress.

Toilet manufacturers have convinced me that some models do work. The excuses they have given me for the problems with early 1.6 gallon models are that they were rushed into construction (not a good excuse, 1.6 gallon has been the standard over in Europe for years), not built to strict ANSI (American National Standards Institute) standards specifications (I'll believe that), cheaply made overseas and improperly glazed (unforgivable if true).

Is There Any Way to Get a 1.6 Gallon Toilet That Works?

The only 1.6 gallon toilets I can guarantee work are those equipped with Flushmate by the Sloan Valve Company, rather than the standard gravity fed water closets.

Baths

The Flushmate is a football sized water tank that fits inside the water closet and expels a 1.5 gallon supply of water at a flush rate of 70 gallons per minute. This extremely high water pressure completely clears the system every time.

The only problems with the system are that it is louder than standard models and prices start in the $200 - $250 price range. Another new system, called the PF/2, invented by R. Bruce Martin, the same man who developed the Flushmate, supposedly takes care of the noise problem. This technology is still in the prototype stages at the time of publication of this book, so all I am passing on is hearsay.

The major manufacturers, American Standard, Crane, Eljer, Gerber, Kohler, Mansfield, and Universal, have Flushmate models. If the PF/2 is as good as they say it is, I am certain that many of these manufacturers will also include this new technology in their line up.

In the meantime, if you buy the 1.6 gallon technology, try to get a guarantee from the supplier that the unit can be returned if it does not flush effectively. If the supplier is willing to give you a sales pitch, but not return privileges. My advice would be to find another supplier, or choose a toilet that you know will be effective.

Baths

What's the Best Way to Replace the Bathtub? The Enameled Surface Is Very Worn in Several Places.

There are three things you can do: reglaze, reline or replace. I am not a fan of reglazing because the resulting surface is very delicate and can be ruined with one application of an abrasive cleaner.

Bathtub Relining

Relining has a lot going for it. It has been a standard practice in the hotel business for years. It is very fast and only about half the cost of replacement. The bathtub relining company comes in takes measurements and custom molds 1/4" thick acrylic high impact polymer to the exact dimensions of your tub.

Don't replace a tub because you don't like the color. A Bathtub Reliner can give you any color you want.

The new tub surface can be just about any color you want. The resulting surface is very hard, almost maintenance free, and keeps water hot up to three times longer than a cast iron tub.

Replacement is the third alternative. Taking the old tub out is a tough job. Usually you have to cut the cast iron tub into three of four pieces before you can man handle the thing out of the bathroom.

Baths

Tub removal also requires replacing the tiles or other tub surround.

If you decide that you are going to replace the tub, I suggest that you consider treating yourself to a whirlpool. A whirlpool is a bargain. You and the family get to enjoy it now and it will help you sell your home when it comes time to move.

Replacement Tubs

If you decide you have to replace the tub, you have three choices: cast iron; enameled steel; and one of the man made tubs: plastic, acrylic, fiberglass or cultured marble.

Cast iron is still the deluxe tub material. Replacement prices start at about $300 (1997 prices). Before you decide that is your choice, make careful measurements. It may well be that your original tub was put in before many of the walls, doorways, and staircases. You might have to take out a wall to put in a new cast iron tub. You probably don't want to do that.

Enameled steel is a good, durable, and inexpensive tub. Prices start at around $125. Unfortunately, enameled steel is prone to damage. If a big dog with long nails gets in the tub, or anything else happens that can scratch the surface, rust starts and eventually the tub has to go.

Baths

The quality of man-made tubs varies enormously. They are light weight and easily to put in place. Prices range from $100 to $500.

When you replace a bathtub you are making a 20 year decision. If you sell you house within that period, the decision you make now, will have an impact on the sale of your house.

In addition to standard tubs, you there are many different kinds of jetted tubs now. Where once these tubs were considered a luxury, they are close to being standard in many new subdivisions. Usually a contractor can put a jetted tub in the same size area as your present tub. If you're still holding back, you should know that in 1991 the most asked for option in new construction was a jetted tub in the master bath area. So go on, indulge. You're not really doing this for yourself, you're just improving the resale value of your house.

If space is short, ask yourself if you really use a bathtub or just take showers. You might be able to replace the tub with a shoulderless shower. In other words, you can put in a floor level unit. Instead of lifting your leg over the side of the tub you just walk in. That is very advantageous.

Baths

Make Sure You Get the Tub You Want

If you love the size and shape of your present tub and just want to replace it, make sure that you actually do replace it with the same size and quality. This is one of the places where a lot of manufacturers cheat. The tubs may look the same but the internal measurements may be different. Don't rely on anyone.

Measure the inside dimensions of your present tub, then measure the inside dimensions of the replacement tub. In many cases, the external dimensions of the new tubs are the same, but the internal dimensions are smaller. You will not be happy unless you have at least as much room in the new tub as you had in the old one.

As far as trademarks are concerned, don't be concerned about the name. Worry about the quality of construction. I would go back to the same type of tub that you presently have in the home. If you have cast iron, replace it with a cast iron tub.

I would suggest that you don't just settle for what you see at the local home center. Go to a few plumbing wholesalers and learn what's out there before you buy. One thing that ticks me off, is when I think I did my homework, and then find I could have gotten a product that has many more features for just a few dollars more, a month after I bought the inferior model. Don't let this happen to you. Remember, you are making a 30 year purchase.

Baths

The other thing I want you to do is upgrade the plumbing in the shower area to install a pressure balancing valve. That way, when somebody flushes the toilet, the temperature of the water in the shower will not change.

Also, when you change the tub and are doing some plumbing work, check up on your water heater. If it is pretty old, or you sometimes run out of hot water while in the shower, upgrade to a quick recovery water heater. The plumber is already there, the extra cost will be very slight. Your increased enjoyment will make the extra cost worth while.

Whirlpool Tubs

Before you decide on a whirlpool tub, go to a few plumbing wholesalers and find out what's out there. There are a lot of differences in design, power, number of jets, etc. Some have different settings from a relatively gentle movement to a real hydro massage. Make sure the one you choose gives you what you desire.

Next, check the water supply. Some top of the line whirlpools have water heaters that keep the water hot. Most do not. By its very nature a whirlpool cools water rapidly. If the whirlpool you select does not have an internal water heater, consider installing a tankless water heater exclusively for that bathroom. That way you never have to fear being chased out of the tub by cold water.

Baths

Help! How Do I Keep Paint or Vinyl Wallpaper Sticking to Bathroom Walls?

I get this question all the time. The solution usually has nothing to do with the walls, the fan, the paint or the wallpaper. It is a ventilation problem. A new exhaust fan pulls 70 to 75 cubic feet per minute (CFM) of air out of the bathroom. The average 5' x 8' bathroom is only 320 cubic feet. The exhaust fan is therefore drawing out an entire room full of air every 4 1/2 minutes. Where does the replacement air come from?

The fan needs a source of dry replacement air to operate effectively. When you close the bathroom door, you cut off the replacement air and the only air the fan is getting is what it can suck from under the bathroom door. When ventilation stops moist air just hangs around.

The solution is to give the bathroom a passive air passage between the bath and the rest of the house. This is done by installing air vents above the bathroom door. Complete instructions are in my first book, *Fix it Fast & Easy!*, tip # 28: **How can I get proper ventilation in the bathroom?**

Baths

Briefly you should cut a hole above the door molding and insert 3" x 7" cold air return toe plates on both sides. The fins should point to the ceiling on the outside wall, and point to the ground on the inside of the bathroom. If a stud is showing behind the toe plates, paint it black. Then, paint the toe plates to match the walls.

What's the Best Way to Replace Shower Tiles?

The first thing you have to decide is whether you really want to tear out the old tile. If you are going to tear out the bath tub, then new tile may be required. If you are not, consider having the tile relined by a bathtub relining company.

Bathtub relining companies can cover the tiles with solid, seamless acrylic surface in the color of your choice. They can also marbleize the walls at a fraction of the cost of real marble.

Since the process completely eliminates the grout and the final surface is perfectly smooth, it is far more difficult for dirt to adhere and the walls are much easier to clean.

Baths

If considerations, like cost, time and mess, are factors, relining is the clear winner. A good bathtub relining company can reline the tub and tiles and be out in a day at a cost that is far less than the replacement alternative. Tearing out and replacing the tile takes days or weeks, and creates a lot more havoc and mess.

The biggest decision is whether you like the look of acrylic. Personally, I think its solid, shiny smoothness is a great look and I love the easy care features. Some people would only be satisfied with the look, texture and design possibilities of tile. If you are one of those, I have to admit that some of the hand fired accent tiles, and tile murals that are being made by craftsmen and women today in just every part of the country can make a dramatic difference.

How Do I Remove Old Wall Tiles & Install New Tiles?

Actual removal can be accomplished rapidly. Quite often, the biggest problem is scheduling the trades. The most important part of the task is deciding what comes after. Make certain that everything is selected and all necessary new materials delivered before the tear out is started.

A deciding factor as to whether you hire some one, or do the job yourself, may be the price of the tile. If you want to do the job yourself and are just using relatively

inexpensive, common wall tile, go for it. If you have selected some of the more expensive tiles, imported tiles, or
for heaven's sake designer tiles, have a professional do the
work. Saving money in these cases is like wanting to do
your own dental work.

You may decide to split the job. You do the tear out
and a professional does the tiling. They are usually so
busy that they are very amenable to this.

You may decide to do the entire job. In that case,
there are some really good books on installing tile. Read
them thoroughly and watch a couple of "How To" videos
on the subject before you start.

If at all possible, I suggest that you go to a large tile
distributor in a major metropolitan area before starting this
job. They will probably have displays which will show
you the complete bathroom tiling project, as well as have
the widest possible assortment of tile samples that you can
use for your project.

They are not going to sell you anything but they
will have literature on the various tiles and will be able to
direct you to retailers who can sell you what you need.
The secret is to learn as much as you can before you start
to tear up the place.

Baths

Tile Removal Instructions for Indomitable Do-It-Yourselfers

Materials needed: Elbow grease

Equipment needed: 4" or 5" Brick Chisel, Ball-peen Hammer or a Small Sledge Hammer, Long Sleeved Shirt, Goggles, Leather Gloves, Wet & Dry Vacuum, Canvas Drop Clothes

If you decide to do the job yourself, you will be surprised at how fast you can tear out the old. You need the right equipment, and you have to protect your eyes and skin from flying tile.

1. Drape the floor with a canvas drop cloth before starting so all the tile just falls onto the tarp and you can haul it to the dumpster, or garbage can easily.

2. To do the job fast, you are going to need a very wide chisel, often called an electrician's brick chisel and a ballpeen hammer or a small sledge hammer. I prefer a small sledge hammer because it is slightly heavier. The weight of the tools, not you, does the work.

You will actually use very little muscle. Just a light swing of the heavy hammer, hitting the chisel does the job. Work from the top down. Your biggest danger will be hitting your hand instead of the chisel, and cutting yourself with flying glass. Remember, flying ceramic is like flying glass. Keep yourself protected with goggles, leather gloves, long sleeved shirt, heavy slacks and shoes, even if it gets hot.

3. When you pull the ceramic off, you will be left with a wood, green board or chicken wire surface. Inspect the plumbing and all wood very carefully.

4. Vacuum up any small debris.

5. Now is the time to make any necessary repairs. If there has been any water damage over the years you may have to replace some of the green board and wood supports.

How Do I Install Ceramic Wall Tile?

If you are meticulous, installing wall tile is easy. Laying out the pattern and cutting the tiles that have to be cut may drive you crazy.

Understand this. Anyone can install ceramic tile. If you are the type who actually enjoys hanging wall paper and can just about do it in your sleep, you will find installing ceramic tile a snap. If you aren't, and you value your sanity, ask the tile retailer for the name of a couple of good installers. There is a reason they can make a good living doing this kind of stuff.

Baths

If you have decided that you want to do the tile installation yourself, ask the tile store for some pamphlets and go to the library and look at a few books on the subject. Home Depot's book, *Home Improvement 1-2-3*[1], and Reader's Digest's *New Complete Do-It-Yourself Manual*[2], have very good sections on ceramic tile installation.

Here are some tips:

1. The wall board surface must be perfectly flat. Any imperfections will be magnified many times over. Be sure to use green board, not regular dry wall.

2. Buy enough extra tile to allow for breakage now, plus create a reserve for problems later. There is nothing more frustrating than to break one tile and not be able to find a same size, same color, same glaze replacement.

3. Be very meticulous. Every line must be exactly level. Don't make guesses or take short cuts.

4. Be sure to make up a tile stick. That is a measuring stick laid out in tile widths. If the tiles are not square, make another tile stick laid out in heights. Allow room for the spacers between tiles.

5. Draw all start and stop lines, and the position of all cabinets, towel racks, soap racks, etc. on the wall.

---

[1] The Home Depot, Home Improvement 1-2-3, 1995, The Merideth Corp., pp. 246 -251.
[2] The Readers Digest Association, Inc., New Complete Do-It-Yourself Manual, 1991, Readers Digest, pp. 312-315.

6. Mark and cut all the wall tiles that you are going to use in an entire row, before beginning the row.

7. Begin installation with the second row up from the bottom, not the bottom row. Be sure to install a temporary support board underneath this row before beginning. This support board will bear the weight of all the wall tile until the tile adhesive has set.

8. If you have a lot of tiles to cut, rent a power tile saw.

How Do I Take Off a Pre-Fabricated Laminated Tub Surround?

Materials needed: Hard Adhesive Remover

Equipment needed: Heat Gun, Pryzem Bar, 1" x 3", Scraper, Sponge Brush.

The laminate comes in three sheets. Some times they were originally put on with paneling adhesive. Paneling adhesive can be activated by heat. If you have a heat gun, see if there is a bead configuration. Heat the adhesive and pull the laminate away.

If they used mastic, heat the laminated surface then pry the panel towards you. The best tool for this job is a flat wrecking bar called a Pryzem. A Pryzem is about 22" in length. It is very flat and it has a nail prong at one end and a curved end on the other end. You can hold it with one hand.

After heating the laminated board, pry one edge up with the Pryzem. The heat dissipates quickly, so hurry.

Pry one edge up, then slide the 1" x 3" behind it. Now slide the Pryzem down some more. Keep working the panel up and pushing the Pryzem and the 1" x 3" farther and farther down. When ever you get stuck, use the heat gun. The problem is getting the heat back there.

After you have pulled off the laminated sheet, you can get rid of the adhesive with Hard Adhesive Remover.

Hard Adhesive Remover works fast. Spread it on, let it set for 20 to 30 minutes, then scrape away. Be sure to use a scraper, not a chisel blade putty knife.

Baths

How Do I Re-Caulk around the Bases of a Toilet, Bathtub & Vanity?

Materials needed: Caulk Remover, Poly Seam Seal, Household Bleach and Rubbing Alcohol,

Equipment needed: Wooden Spoon or Plastic Putty Knife, Old Tooth Brush, Gloves, Goggles, EZ Caulker,

You should remove all the old caulk. This doesn't have to be a hassle. 3M has a product called Caulk Remover. You can squirt that all over everything. Be patient. It takes about 2 hours to really break down the grip of the old caulk. Remove the old caulk with an old wooden spoon or a plastic putty knife.

After you remove the old caulk, take some rubbing alcohol or bleach and wash the area down. Rub it down thoroughly. The alcohol breaks the grip of soap and takes away any residue.

To recaulk, use a vinyl or one of the elastromeric caulks. They are simple to use. They smooth out easily. You'll also find a little tool called the E-Z Caulker at the hardware store. This little tool is all that it takes to make your caulk lines look like they were done by a professional.

Baths

Another tool is made by Myro. They make the tool where you put your index finger in the little piece of plastic and it has a groove in it and you just pull it along the bead line.

Myro also makes caulker tips that you can slide over the caulking tube to make different sized beads. It is inexpensive.

Here's how to do the project.

1. Fill the tub half full of cold water. The reason for doing this is that the weight of the water pulls the tub down and away from the wall slightly, giving you the widest gap to caulk.

2. Remove the old caulk.

3. Clean away all residue with bleach and a toothbrush. Throw the toothbrush away when you are done.

4. Rinse with clear water and let it dry. Keep the water in the tub at all times.

5. Let dry, then wash the dry area with rubbing alcohol.

6. Caulk the surface.

7. Leave the water in the tub for an hour and a half after caulking to let the caulk set.

Baths

Later on, if you believe mold and mildew will become a problem, pour some full strength vinegar on rag and wipe the caulk bead every once in a while. Vinegar is a preventative. Make that part of your weekly cleaning ritual.

If the mildew is growing, remove it with X-14, or Mildew Stain Remover.

I'm Renovating My 30 Year Old Bathroom. It Has Linoleum on the Floor. I Want to Replace It with Ceramic Tile. What Should I Replace? What Should I Keep?

You and your conscience have to decide on the tub and the tile. Everything else goes. Blow out the toilet. Get a new vanity and upgrade the sink. When you pull up the linoleum, the underlayment has to be clean before you put anything else down.

Baths

How Do I Tear Up the Linoleum?

**Materials needed: Adhesive Remover by Citristrip, 3/4"
Plywood, Drywall Screws for Sub Floor.**

**Equipment needed: Strong back, strong knees, two
month's supply of elbow grease, Hand Operated Slammer
Scraper by Werner, Gloves, Circular Saw, Drill, Screw-
driver.**

1. Take out the vanity. Take everything out of the bath-
    room before you start removing the linoleum. The
    only thing I want you to have on the floor is the
    flange where the toilet sat. Seal the flange with a bag
    or put rags over the top to block the odor.

2. Removing linoleum is a two man job. The best way
    to do it is to rent or buy a hand operated Floor Tile
    Slammer Scraper.

    One person uses the tool to pry up the linoleum
while the other person peels it lose.

3. Remove any adhesive that has remained stuck to the
    sub floor with Adhesive Remover by Citristrip.

4. The 3/4" plywood that you are going to see under-
    neath the linoleum is called the underlayment. It
    must be in really good shape before you put down
    the ceramic floor. Anywhere that you see water
    damage or rot, get a circular saw and cut out the bad
    wood.

Baths

You will probably have to replace much of the sub floor. Attach with drywall screws. Before tile installation begins, the sub floor must be rigid and absolutely level with no squeaks.

Underlayment

It is best at this time to apply a new underlayment. This is a critical part of this job. I recommend US Gypsum's Durock cement board. It must be absolutely secure with no squeaks. There can be no squeaks, so do not space the screws more than 6" apart on the center seams.

You are now ready to lay down the flooring of your choice.

Treat the whole room as a wet installation. That means, use water resistant adhesives and Silicone Caulk by Dow or GE Silicone II.

My Bathroom Floor Has Small, 1" x 1" Tiles in the Bathroom. I Want to Put in a New Tile Floor. Can I Do the Job Myself or Should I Have Some One Else Do It? What Do I Do?

I, personally, would call in a good ceramic tile person. You can lay your own ceramic tile if you want to. The same thing I said about installing ceramic wall tile

Baths

applies here. There are quite a few books on the subject and most tile suppliers also provide detailed instructions for the novice tile layer. Be very meticulous and have your pattern laid out before you start.

Your present ceramic tile floor makes an excellent base. Just make certain that you use water-proof floor adhesive. Spread it on with a serrated metal trowel with 3/8" serrations and place the tile into the adhesive.

I guarantee that you will be bragging about this job for a long, long time.

Chapter 6
Room Additions

Room Additions

How to Design & Plan Room Additions

Room additions are the ultimate way to make your home conform to your changing needs. They tell me that people are happy with their communities and want to keep their roots while growing and building for the future.

At the same time, as a homeowner, you have to be careful about whether your proposed addition fits in with the house and the surrounding neighborhood, or there may not be sufficient return on the dollar when it comes time to sell your home.

Too many people think only about the inside. The exterior look is just as important as the interior. If it takes away from your home's appearance, it will reduce salability, no matter how nice and snug it is inside.

Architects

Don't be afraid to consider hiring an architect to plan your addition. "Free plans" are nice, but many times they are worth even less than you pay for them. Chances are that if the remodeling salesperson or contractor knew enough to be a licensed architect, they would be a licensed architect.

Room Additions

This is not to say that many fine remodeling companies do not have excellent design departments, they do. Many, however, are staffed by kids with no initials after their names. They may be conscientious, but they are just doing a job and wouldn't know state of the art if they were looking at it.

Builders and remodeling sales people are in business to make a buck giving you what you want. Their prime concern is to be cost effective (for themselves, maybe even for you), and they are eminently practical.

If that's what you want, a good modernization contractor can give it to you. If you want to stretch the envelope, why not give a chance to a guy or gal who is not only trained, but actually gets his or her jollies out of doing just that, a licensed architect.

Keep in mind that architects are not builders. Pretty is more important than practical, and their main focus is not the cost of items, so budgets may get bumped. Some large builders try to have the best of both worlds and have a licensed architect on staff.

One proviso. In most cases when dealing with independent architects, you just want to brainstorm with them and get a set of plans that you can use to get bids from various contractors. You do not want them to oversee the entire job. Unless your job is very technical, they don't usually add much supervision, can cloud matters of liability if a problem occurs, and often get a piece of the action of all construction costs, meaning you get a bigger bill.

Room Additions

Don't Mix Styles

Back to basics. If you have a brick home, try to match the brick when you build a ground level addition. If the home is Tudor or Californian, make sure that the addition is a complimentary style.

Sun rooms can add interest, but they are usually quite expensive because of all the tempered glass. If the reason for the addition is to shelter a spa, it's a great idea. But be careful, an enclosed spa area should have its own heating, cooling and ventilation or it will spread an amazing amount of humidity throughout the house.

Dormer additions can enhance or destroy the look of a house. Skillfully done they turn a bungalow into a colonial. Badly designed, they can give a house an unbalanced look that makes you think the house will collapse of its own weight.

If you only need to add one bedroom, don't just add a clump to the left or right side of the house. Center the room, or better still, extend the addition to include the entire width of the house.

If you want, you can build a large addition but only finish the interior of the room that's needed. You'll be surprised how soon the family will let you know they need more growing room. Even unfinished, an extra room can be a big selling point.

Room Additions

Back to Basics

It is usually quite easy to extend the plumbing service to a new addition, but electrical, heating and cooling systems may be a problem. Make certain that the new addition has plenty of electric power. If the rest of the house is under powered, this might be a perfect time to upgrade the electrical service for the entire house.

Check with the heating and cooling contractor to make certain that your home's present heating and cooling plant has sufficient capacity to extend to the addition. No one wants to pay the extra money, and a remodeling sales-man will often not want to bring it up, but additional heating and cooling systems are often required if the new rooms are not going to be too cold in winter, and too hot in summer.

So far everything you have done has been need and emotion based. "The kids are getting older and need a room of their own." "The house is too confining, we need a family room and an extra bath." "Mother is coming to live with us and she needs a bedroom, sitting room, kitch-enette and bath." Always with the proviso, "we like the schools, community and neighbors, and do not want to move."

Room Additions

That is wonderful. It means you have a stable community and a happy home. But before you sign on the proverbial dotted line, it's a good idea to study all the alternatives.

Is It Worth the Effort?
Cost Vs Value Analysis

Find out what your house is worth in the present market. Then add the price of the addition. Let's say your present house is worth $185,000. The addition will come to $50,000. Doesn't it just make good sense to see how much of house you can buy for $235,000 before committing to the addition?

You may find that you couldn't duplicate the house and addition for $275,000. That makes the addition one heck of a deal. On the other hand, you might find that you could get the house of your dreams in a brand new subdivision for the same amount of money, or that there is a house a mile away with everything you need for only $200,000. In that case, even if you pay $5,000 to move, you still save $30,000. Wouldn't that money look better invested in growth mutual funds than in the builder's account?

Room Additions

Mother-In-Law Additions

Mother-in-law additions are quite expensive to build. At time of resale they are hard to get a dollar for dollar return, because they are atypical. If you are lucky, and some one is selling, at the same time you need the additional room, you may find that you can duplicate most of the features of your present house, plus the mother in law wing, and still save $25 to $50,000 over the cost of adding on to your own home. That is sad for the seller, but if someone has to lose the money, wouldn't you prefer that it be the other guy, not you?

You may decide that regardless of the money, you choose to stay where you are. I applaud that decision. America would be a better place if we had more homeowners like you.

I'm Making My Unheated Attic Into Bedrooms. Any Tips?

Making use of the room you already have can save a lot of money. How you decorate is up to you. From a practical stand point, the two magic ingredients are insulation and air handling. You can install loose or fiberglass batt insulation on the floors in the unheated eaves, fiberglass batts or rigid foam insulation on the knee walls and under the roof.

Room Additions

Remember, just because you are putting rooms up there doesn't mean that you can cut off the roof's air circulation. The roof has to breath. That means you need soffit vents for incoming air, soffit baffles to assure that the insulation doesn't block the soffit vents. You also need ridge vents, for outgoing air. Install rafter baffles or vents directly under the roof. This will provide convenient air passages between the roof decking and the insulation.

As far as heating the new attic rooms, the work must be done by a good heating contractor. He has the know-how to tell whether your present furnace is big enough to heat the two new rooms. He will also install the necessary new insulated ductwork.

Make certain that he installs a minimum of one hot air register and two louvered, cold air returns per room. The contractor may argue about two cold air returns, but you need them. I'll tell you why in a minute. The hot air register goes on the floor. One cold air return at the ceiling line, one at floor level.

You will have to pay a little extra for the second cold air return and louvered, rather than unlouvered, models. Attic rooms can get notoriously hot in the summer and cold in the winter. Hot air rises, cold air sinks. During the winter when you want to keep as much hot air as possible, you close the top cold air return and send the cold floor air back to the furnace for re-heating. During the summer, when you want as much cool air as possible, you close the bottom cold air return and open the top. This draws the hot ceiling air down to the air conditioning unit to be chilled, and leaves the relatively cool floor level air in the room.

Is Building a Dormer a Good Idea?

Building up, not out, can be a great idea. Believe it or not, Adam Helfman's (the builder I quoted in the second chapter) grandfather, Philip, and Philip's brother, Leroy, invented and held a patent on the modern dormer. People have been building up since the stone age. The Helfmans' concept was the "floating" dormer, a way to set new joists on the existing structure, making construction much faster and cost effective.

Properly done, building up instead of out can save time, money, and add space and value to your house. Improperly done, it can literally ruin it. The home's architectural look and structural integrity can be destroyed.

Speed and timing is critical. You want to know that the crew working on your house is fast and good. The first thing they have to do is "open" your house. That means that much or all of the roof is removed, leaving the house at the mercy of the elements. A sudden rain, combined with an untrained or uncaring crew, can deluge the house with water, ruining insulation, ceiling mounted electrical, and drywall or plaster.

Room Additions

I would never allow a crew to start a tear off on my house unless they were equipped with several heavy duty tarps. In the event of a sudden storm, I would want to make sure my house could be protected. If you are having a dormer built, have the radio tuned to the local station that gives the best weather reports and keep looking up at the sky. Your house is vulnerable until the new walls and roof are up.

As far as structural integrity is concerned, I've heard of jobs where members of the crew literally fell through the roof and destroyed the furniture in the rooms below. Rotten decking aside, the arch of the roof rafters provides support for the walls. When you remove the roof you take away much of the wall support. This is a lot like brain surgery. Perfectly do-able, but no place for amatures.

I don't want anything written here to frighten you away from having a dormer built on your house. I do want to frighten you enough to make you understand that the crew has to be very experienced. Just good carpenters won't do. You have to see several dormers they have built and talked to the homeowners to make certain that the work was done fast and that they experienced no problems.

Room Additions

Check Your Homeowner's Insurance

It also means that you have to be very particular about insurance. Imagine if the impossible happened. A workman fell through the first floor ceiling and it rained. Who would pay the damages? The workman was either injured or killed. Who pays for the workman's comp or death benefits? In the case of severe injury, we could be talking hundreds of thousands of dollars. If the builder does not have sufficient insurance, the homeowner is responsible.

In the above scenario, your house would also have experienced thousands of dollars of damage. Who would bring the existing home up to its former condition? If the builder didn't have sufficient insurance and didn't have the desire or the money to make the repairs and finish the job, it would be up to your home owner's insurance and you.

Need I add that this is not a situation where you can let everything hang for six months or a year while you get a judge to do something about solving your problem? Building a dormer, room addition, or any major home modernization, is definitely a time you need to huddle with your homeowner's insurance agent and have an umbrella rider that will provide you and your home the necessary protection in case of an emergency.

Room Additions

Advice from a Building Inspector

Let me conclude this chapter by passing on some of the advice a seasoned building inspector, Pat Murphy, told an audience at a remodeling seminar I gave a few years ago. Pat is a real pro and he spoke about the real world of remodeling.

He warned the homeowners, never to apply for a building permit unless they were going to do the work themselves or not to try to "save money" by not taking out a permit. Every year, thousands, maybe millions of homeowners get taken in by these fringe builder cons.

The person who applies for the permit is responsible for the job. If you apply for the permit, or even worse, don't apply for a permit, the responsibility rests entirely with you.

If the Building Department learns that work is in process, that was not approved, they have the power to stop the job and hold it up until a permit is applied for and received.

Even worse, when it comes time to sell your house, in many localities, if the work was not approved, the Building Department during a pre-sale inspection can order you to tear open the job, so that they can make the required inspections. When this happens it can easily cost you thousands of dollars in aggravation, lower resale value, and lost buyers.

Room Additions

Pat also told the audience to make sure their new construction was livable. "One of the biggest causes of homeowner remorse, is that they try to save a few dollars by cutting the size of a room and wind up with a cramped area that just makes them unhappy," he said.

This is really good advice. Remember, all the pressure to build is being generated by you. Don't build unless you can afford it. When you do, build the job right, so you will be pleased for many years to come.

Pat also cautioned homeowners that living through remodeling was the acid test of a marriage. "Expect severe stress. If you can't live with it, don't remodel." Another tip, "expect a mess, no matter what they promise, the building trades seldom clean up after themselves."

Murphy's final bit of advice was never to assume that a proposed remodeling job is in compliance with zoning laws just because the contractor, or designer, says it is.

"Every municipality is different. What is perfectly legal in the next town, may be against an ordinance where you live. If the job is out of compliance, you need to get a variance from the Zoning Board. That can set back your job four or five months, and there is no guarantee that the variance will be granted," Pat Murphy said.

Room Additions

The chances are that if you had an opportunity to sit down and have a beer with a senior building inspector where you live, he'd give you the same advice. My suggestion is that you put a book mark at the beginning of these last few paragraphs and read them over before you start any remodeling job.

Chapter 7
Basements

Basements

Going from Soggy to Sensational

Basements are an enigma. On the one hand, they are a home owner's largest single repository of available space. Space that makes people with houses built on slabs and crawl spaces salivate with envy.

This space can be relatively easily and economically remodeled into anything you need. A recreation room, bedroom, office, hobby room, or a combination of all of these, is available with a minimum of effort or expense.

Unfortunately, the basement's spatial bounty is often confounded by the basement's second, and far less appealing, characteristic. Your basement is a puddle waiting to happen. The only reason that it is ever dry is that your buddy, the builder, lined it with six inches of cement, put in some drainage tiles and built a house over it. Otherwise it would be just a hole waiting for rain and water flow to make it a palace for pollywogs.

Mother nature has eternity. Over time, fill land settles, concrete block and poured concrete walls crack, drainage tiles are invaded by roots, plugged by debris, and crumble with age. Slowly, but surely, Mother Nature works to regain the upper hand and make your basement the puddle it was meant to be.

Basements

Why Basements Get Wet

Water moves through building materials and into the house in four different ways: liquid flow, capillary suction, convection, and diffusion.

Liquid Flow is exemplified by the leaks we all know and love.

Capillary suction is caused by the ability of the concrete to "wick" moisture through the medium. The asphalt smeared on the exterior of the basement walls stops that. If the covering breaks down, capillary action will start.

Water vapor is transported by air movement or convection. This is primarily a problem in the attic, not the basement.

Diffusion results when water vapor passes through small pores in the concrete or other building materials. This is the flip side of convection. It is rarely a problem in the upper portions of the house, but is a prime reason for damp, humid basements when no leaks are present.

If you want to spoil Mother Nature's plan, and not let her turn your basement into a palace for pollywogs, the price you must pay is eternal vigilance.

Basements

Sixty percent of basement problems are caused by the slope of the ground outside your house. Over the years the house settles, ground settles, you change the landscaping, a misdirected down spout directs water toward the foundation or washes ground away, cement heaves or settles directing water toward the house.

Make a plan to take an inspection tour around the house every couple of months. A good time to check is when it is raining so you can watch Mother Nature in action. Check to see where bird bathing (puddles) are occurring near the foundation. Watch the water run off. See where the roof gutters are uneven, causing water to collect and overflow the gutters instead of being directed to the down spouts.

Write down where the problems are occurring. Then correct them as soon as it is dry.

How Do You Stop Basements From Leaking?

I've really been repeating the answer over and over again throughout this entire section of the chapter. **You have to put your basement on a water-free diet.**

Basements

The Difference Between Poured Concrete & Concrete Block Basements

Poured concrete is a porous solid. Concrete block is a porous solid formed into a hollow block. In extremely wet conditions hydrostatic pressure forces water into the wall, filling the hollow blocks. Even when the ground becomes dry, the wall will leak until all the water has drained out of the blocks.

On the other hand, both concrete block and poured concrete walls can be insulated very easily with Dow or Amoco 1" thick foam boards to provide a warm and snug basement.

Removing Efflorescence before Painting

The white powder on the concrete is called efflorescence. It is a by product of water. What is happening is that where the wall gets damp after a real heavy rain and then dries out, it leaves behind mineral deposits.

A temporary fix is to wash the efflorescence away. The only way to solve the problem is to put your basement on a water free diet. As we discussed earlier, increase the grade of the ground around the house, so that water washes away and does not soak into the soil.

Basements

After you have solved the moisture problem, and the wall had dried out, here's how to prepare and paint the concrete surface.

Materials needed: TSP, UGL Drylock or Perma White by Zinsser.

Equipment needed: Buckets, 2 Long Handled Scrub Brush; Goggles, Rubber Gloves, Cement Brush

To clean off the efflorescence use TSP solution and a scrub brush.

1. Mix four ounces dry measure of TSP to a gallon of warm water. Scrub the surface with a scrub brush. This is a very strong cleaning solution. Be sure to wear goggles, rubber gloves and a long sleeved shirt and slacks.

2. Rinse the surface copiously with clear water.

3. Let dry 24 hours.

4. Paint with either UGL Drylock or Zinsser Perma White. These two paints are ready mix basement wall paints. They are specialty formulated so that if that moisture comes back the paint will not be adversely affected. They let the alkalinity pass through rather than fight it and peel again.

Basements

The secret to successful concrete painting is to really work the first coat into the wall. You will only get about a 150 square feet per gallon.

Decorating the basement, turning it into a rec room, or what ever, comes next. Because of the area's special attributes, the procedures called for are a little different than decorating any other room.

How Do I Make Certain a Basement Will Never Flood?

Easy. Put it on stilts on top of a mountain. Any other technique leaves you at the mercy of the elements. However, if you want to be 99% sure that your basement will never flood, you can do the following:

1. Make sure all prior leaks have been thoroughly repaired before beginning to finish the basement.

2. Keep checking for proper exterior water drainage.

3. I assume your basement already has a sump pump. If not, install one. Then install a water powered back up sump pump so that the sump continues to be drained even when there is an electric power outage.

4. Install an interior drain tile system so that if the exterior storm drain tile system ever fails (and it almost always does) your basement will be protected by a back up system.

Basements

An interior drain tile system includes the installation of 4" PVC drain pipes underneath the cement slab and easy to get to clean outs so that the entire system can be cleaned on a regular basis.

The interior drain tile system and all other methods of basement waterproofing are covered in the special basement waterproofing in *Fix It Fast & Easy 3, Frantic Fixes!*

Basements

Sensational Basements

Basement remodeling is a non-issue for most of the people living in the Southern and Western parts of the United States. If your house was built on a slab or crawl space, the rest of this chapter is not for you. You may want to read it for general interest, or to find how the other half lives. Some of the cement floor insulation tips may be helpful.

For those of us lucky enough to live in the North, East, Midwest, Central and Rocky Mountain regions, basements are a bonanza we wouldn't be without.

Along with the living area and attic area, the basement is one of the three main envelopes of the house. It has its own atmosphere. It is cooler than the rest of the living area. It was meant to be that way. After all, basements are just designed to be places to put the mechanicals (water heater, furnace, laundry tubs) and storage. Air circulation is accidental.

Naturally, being human, most people are not content to leave basements to their assigned duties. We want to turn them into living space.

If you aspire to better things, it is hard not to build up the basement. When Barb and I built our house a few years ago, the basement had only a furnace room and storage. Suddenly, I had all that space. It seemed a sin to waste it, so Barb, Eric, and Heather, set up an office and work area.

A year went by, my earlier interest in fine wines blossomed into a hobby and I built a wine cellar. Later, my desire to enjoy an occasional fine cigar with a glass of vintage port without going outside or getting nasty looks from the rest of the family, convinced me that what I really needed was a smoking room.

Now, I've have the basement of my dreams. Only problem is, I need to rent storage space at one of those "Grandmother's Attic" self storage places.

I described this ridiculous scenario because I wanted you to know that nothing you might like to do is any crazier than what I have already done. You have my permission to go crazy, too. But here are a few ground rules.

Basement Basics

First: the furnace is usually the prime tenant in the basement. The furnace needs room to breath. Do not just close it off and expect it to function properly. The furnace area must have unrestricted ventilation, and be big enough so that repairs and eventual replacement can be easily accomplished.

Second: if the laundry area is downstairs, make sure it retains the room, light, and ventilation it needs.

Basements

Third: make sure that your basement is bone dry, and that the walls and slab are in excellent condition before you even think of remodeling.

Fourth: swear yourself to a life of eternal vigilance against exterior bird-bathing, erosion, and cement tilts. Water collecting around your basement walls spells danger at any time. If you have remodeled your basement and installed carpeting, a computer or expensive furnishings, it can be a disaster.

I Want To Put an Office and a Rec Room in My Basement. Is Ceiling Tile Necessary?

Historically ceiling tiles have been the way to go. They have been vastly improved over the years. However, while they help to give the basement a very finished look, they take away from ceiling height and may be an expense you do not need.

Height is always a problem unless you are blessed with an especially deep basement. If a truly "finished look" is not a necessity, not covering the first floor joists can give the impression of greater height. If such is the case, you might try painting or staining the floor joists and first floor underlayment instead of adding a dropped ceiling.

Painting everything overhead including all the pipes a flat white will make the pipes fade from view. The white color will help lighten even the darkest basement.

Basements

On the other hand, those floor joists are an open invitation to install recessed lighting that gives light without cutting back on head room.

You might also want to consider installing dry wall on the ceiling and walls. Combined with recessed lighting, the drywall gives the basement a finished look that can not be duplicated in any other way.

People with walk out basements, or basements with eight or nine feet high ceilings, do not really have basements at all. They have an additional level of living space that was meant to be finished off like conventional rooms.

What Are The Easiest and Most Economical Ways to Treat the Basement Walls and Floors?

It all depends upon whether you're a bachelor or are married. Stop, don't hit me. Some people do not mind a rather rustic look. They don't care if it's cool. They don't expect to do a lot of living down there. They just want the basement to look sort of presentable for the one or two times a year they have a blast and need the extra room. Let's call these people bachelors.

Basements

Other people want to create a warm, cozy, living space they, or their children, can use all the time. They want, or need, more living space. We'll call them married.

Bachelors can get by with a good TSP wash down of the walls and floors. I recommend 4 oz. dry measure of TSP or Dirtex to every gallon of hot water. Scrub into the concrete with a pole mounted brush, then rinse copiously. Change rinse water often. Remember to protect yourself with goggles, long sleeved shirt and rubber gloves when you do this.

Painting Basement Walls

The next step up would be painting the walls. If you want to do that, set up oscillating fans to keep the air moving and let the walls and floor dry for a week. Then patch any scaling with a good vinyl cement patcher and paint the walls with a good cement paint like UGL Drylock or Perma White by Zinsser.

Floors can be left as is, or etched with a muratic acid solution and stained with any good cement stain. If you etch the floor take all the necessary precautions. Remember, muratic acid is inexpensive and can be purchased at any hardware store. It can also burn your skin. Even breathing in the vapors can do permanent damage to your lungs. It can blind your eyes, and, last but not least, kill you.

Basements

I hope that I have frightened you enough so that you will wear long sleeved shirts, pants, rubber gloves, goggles and a respirator equipped with canisters rated for harsh chemicals. Set up fans and open windows because you will need to exchange the air constantly.

The next step up is using something like Bondex Texture Paint or an extra thick version of a basement cement paint on the walls with a loop textured roller and then creating a texture by combing, brushing, sponge swirling, or using a spackling knife to make a pattern by building up layers of paint.

Painting Basement Floors

I do not recommend painting basement floors. There are several excellent concrete paint systems on the market, but they are a lot more expensive and cost more than any sane bachelor would want to shell out for a place he is only going to use two or three times a year.

I must warn you here, that if you start going crazy like this, you are very close to making the transition from bachelorhood to the married state. If this is the case and you have reached the time of life, the nesting urge is setting in big time. Better start devoting full time to looking for the all important other half. You can fix up the basement later.

Basements

That being said there are many things you can do if you want to turn your basement into another living area. You can add insulation and put up drywall or paneling. You can paint or wallpaper. Floors can be insulated, tiled, carpeted, even covered with hardwood flooring.

How Do You Make The Basement Feel Like Part of The Living Area?

If you need additional living space, sitting on top of an unfinished basement is like living in a tent pitched on top of buried treasure. Getting your basement finished only costs a fraction of what it would cost to build up or out.

Unfortunately, most finished basements are just that, finished basements. They never become an accepted, fully functioning, part of the house. Since they do not become true living space, they add only marginal resale value to the home.

To find a way around these problems, I talked to Mike McCoy of Coy Construction, Inc., a suburban Detroit builder. Coy specializes in building decks and finishing basements. The company will build 800 decks and finish about 60 basements this year. I do not know of any other contractor in the United States that finishes that many basements.

Basements

McCoy says the secret to getting full use and resale value out of a basement is to change the look and feel from a basement to that of another living level.

The standard way to finish a basement is to put in furring strips and paneling, install a drop ceiling with ugly ceiling tiles, and lay vinyl on the floor.

You would never live in a house with a living room that looked like that. How can you expect to use a basement that looks that way? According to McCoy, to get maximum "living appeal" from a basement, you have to start at the top of the stairs and rethink the entire situation.

When a contractor builds a house he separates the unfinished basement from finished living space with a door at the top of very utilitarian stairs. The door and the stairway combine to tell you "Stop. You don't want to go down there."

To change your basement into living space, get rid of the psychological stop signs. Take out the door and door trim, and open up the staircase by removing as much of the stairway wall as possible. Replace it with a top quality banister that looks exactly like one you would choose for a stairway leading from the front vestibule to the second floor.

Basements

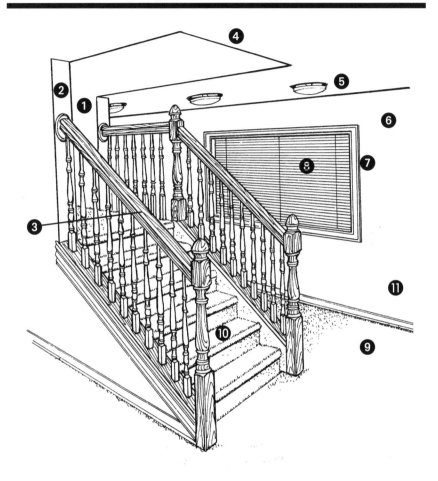

Ways to Make a Basement Look Like Living Space
1) Remove door; 2) Remove stairwell wall; 3) Install a
deluxe rail system; 4) Drywall the ceiling; 5) Install recessed lighting; 6) Drywall walls; 7) Install picture windows between rooms to give an open feel; 8) Install mini-
blinds for privacy when desired; 9) Install deluxe carpeting on floors; 10) Install deluxe carpeting or hardwood
stairs; 11) Hide stanchions in walls.

Basements

By doing these things the staircase becomes a natural progression to a lower living level. You can continue this feel by making the finished portion of the basement look and feel as much like the first floor as possible.

McCoy recommends dry walling both the walls and the ceiling, carpeting, not tiling the floors, adding a full, not a half, bath, recessed lighting and upgrading the electrical by installing at least three additional electric circuits.

By drywalling, instead of installing a drop ceiling, you change the look from industrial to regular room, gain three to four inches in height, giving the basement a much more livable feel; and replace expensive, likely to go out of style and become irreplaceable, ceiling tiles, with inexpensive, easy to replace, drywall. You also gain the flexibility of being able to build around duct work, and save about 60% on materials.

Installing drywall instead of paneling on the walls, accomplishes much the same thing. Since McCoy believes that straight walls are very important, he recommends using full 2" x 4" studs with bottom and top plates, instead of just using furring strips tacked to poured or block basement wall. Naturally, because, there is always a potential for water, the bottom plates have to be pressure treated and drywall should be rated for below ground construction.

Basements

The use of 2" x 4" studs not only gives you the support necessary for a perfectly level drywall surface, instead of the wavy wall usually associated with paneled basements, it also gives extra room for insulation.

Drywall has another advantage, in the event a leak develops, it is very easily and inexpensively replaced. If paneling is used, it becomes almost impossible to duplicate after only a few years.

If you worry about leaks, you may want to consider hanging the 2" x 4"'s from the rafters and not anchoring them to the floor. McCoy's way gives a more finished look, but hanging the studs leaves a safety valve for drainage in case a leak develops.

If you prefer to use furring strips instead of 2" x 4" construction, WALLMATE insulation by DOW USA is especially made with indentations for the strips..

Using carpeting instead of vinyl goods on the floor gives the basement a finished, more comfortable feel. McCoy warns that you should be careful to buy the same quality carpeting you would select for your living room. Even the best indoor-outdoor carpeting gives the room an industrial feel.

If you want to add extra warmth, install Envira Cushion imported by Fairway Tile and Carpet[1] instead of normal padding. It is waterproof and is the only padding I know that lists an R Factor.

---

[1] See Appendix for Supplier Phone List.

Basements

Here are a few other tips for making a finished basement into a natural feeling living area.

1. Lay out the floor plan so that metal stanchions are hidden inside walls.

2. Use the same floor and ceiling moldings in the basement that are used on the first floor.

3. Think about putting in a large fixed window between rooms to provide an open feel.

4. Don't finish the entire basement. Remember, unfinished storage space is a very valuable commodity.

What's The Easiest Way to Install R Value and Drywall?

WALLMATE by DOW USA. It is an extruded Styrofoam product especially designed for basement walls. WALLMATE comes in 8 foot sections, specially cut on the edges to accept 1" x 3" furring strips.

1. Draw straight lines on the concrete for the WALLMATE. Then attach the furring strips into the concrete through the WALLMATE with cement screws.

Basements

2. Attach the drywall or paneling to the furring strips. Make sure that the drywall or paneling is rated for below grade installation.

This method of insulation is a way to get some insulation qualities and a nice looking paneling in about one third of the time as installing a traditional stud wall system.

How Do I Even Out a Stud Wall Over Irregular Concrete Walls?

Build your stud wall inside, but not attached to the wall. Hang the stud wall 24" on centers using 2" x 4"'s from the floor joists. Use a plumb line to make certain that it is absolutely straight, then anchor it with a pressure treated base plate fastened to the floor with cement screws.

The 2" x 4"'s should be hung 3/8" away from the wall. Put fiberglass insulation between the stud walls and run the electrical in front of it. Poly wrapped fiberglass insulation would be my first choice. It is rated R15 or R16. Do not use plastic on the walls below grade as a vapor barrier.

A lot of people with damp basements use duplex nails on the bottom so that they can make the bottom of the wall about a 16th of an inch off the floor.

Basements

What Insulation Should I Use with 2" x 4" Studs?

Since you are going to use 2 x 4's you are not going to go with a WALLMATE system, fiberglass insulation is the best choice.

I am going to repeat my warning against using plastic sheathing as a vapor barrier. Some building inspectors will insist on plastic. Try to explain to the building inspector that plastic or Visqueen below grade is obsolete. In some States it is already against code.

The reason for this is that if you use plastic or Visqueen you will end up with a musty odor after several years and have to pull the paneling off and remove the insulation and plastic because you will find mold growing beneath the plastic.

To keep that problem from happening, you can use faced 3 1/2" thick Batt insulation. That will give you an R 11; or better still, use a Poly wrapped fiberglass insulation. That will give you an R rating of 15 or 16.

Basements

How Do I Level Out The Slope on the Basement Floor Yet Still Keep Access To The Floor Drains?

Depending on the condition of the floor there are three different ways you can build up the slab to make it even or box the slab to provide an even floor surface.

If You Have an Unpainted Old Concrete Floor:

The easiest solution is to build up the concrete to the level you desire. Most of the concrete self leveling products on the market are only effective when the slope is 1 1/2" or less. Since your basement floor slopes 3", use a product called Super Strength Vinyl Patcher by the Quikrete people.

Quikrete Super Strength Vinyl Patcher is a material we call a finish grade. It is a fine powder and comes in 40 LB bags.

1. Clean the concrete surface thoroughly.

2. Mix the Super Strength Vinyl Patcher with water right in the basement, using a hoe, bucket and wheel barrow .

3. Wheel the mix to the work area and trowel it off. You can work with it from a 16th of a inch up to as thick as three or four inches. Super Strength Vinyl Patcher

Basements

already has the compounds in it to make the concrete stick to concrete.

What really makes this product different is that it is finish grade. The aggregate is like dust. When you are finished troweling, you're done.

If the floor has been painted, you can not build it up with Super Strength Vinyl Patcher, because it will not adhere. You have to either completely remove the paint layer and provide a completely new surface for the Vinyl Patcher or build a floor support, called a box, to make the floor level.

If You Have a Painted Floor:

So much of the paint has been absorbed into the concrete, that it is impossible to remove with a chemically based paint remover. It must be sanded. This is not a job for the Do It Yourselfer.

A few specialized companies do this type of work. They have special sanding machines that sands all the paint off the floor. Your best bet is to call concrete suppliers and get the names of contractors who do this kind of work in your area.

If You Want to Box the Floor:

The final alternative is to put in a floor box. You would run sleepers and then 3/4" 4' x 8' sheets of plywood. Here's how to do it.

Basements

1. Clean floor with a solution of 4 oz. dry measure TSP per gallon of water. Rinse well.

2. Let dry a minimum of 1 or 2 days. Open basement windows and use fans during drying time.

3. Lay down pressure treated 2" x 4"'s as sleepers. The 2" x 4" s should start 1/2" from the walls and be placed 16" On Center (OC). The pressure treated wood should be rated at a minimum of .40 CCA (Chromated Cooper Arsenate). .60 CCA is preferred.

   Use shims under the 2" x 4" s to level floors. Some of these shims will be very substantial because you are building up to 3". Cut the shims made from .60 CCA pressure treated wood.

4. Lay down 3/4" exterior plywood for the sub floor. Cut the first panel of every other row to stagger sub floor joints. Leave a 1/4" to 1/2" air space between the plywood and the walls. Keep a space of at least 1/16" between plywood panels.

   Screw the plywood down every 4 to 6" on center.

5. Complete the floor to your specifications.

Basements

I Want to Carpet The Basement Floor. What Type of Insulation Should I Put Down First?

The coldest part of any basement is the floor. Many families want to use the basement for their children's play area but are afraid of the cold. Tile doesn't help. Carpet helps a little bit, but you need something more on a cold winter's evening. Carpet padding doesn't list an R factor.

I would recommend a product called Comfort Base by the Homosote Company and is available at many lumber yards throughout the US; or Envira Cushion, a Mexican made product that is being imported by Fairway Tile and Carpet of Clawson, Michigan.

Comfort Base is comes in 1/2 inch thick 4' x 4' sheets. It provides a much warmer carpet foundation than normal padding.

Envira Cushion comes in 54" widths and is a very dense pad, with a 4.5 R factor.

This new product is 100% odorless, non-toxic, and waterproof. It is impervious to even dog or cat urine. It should make the basement a far more comfortable place.

The only bad thing I have heard about this product is that it is reported to have a tendency to retain denting caused by high heels and heavy furniture. I would seri-

Basements

ously consider this new padding if I were remodeling my basement.

Although distribution is sparse, the far improved R factor makes it the padding of choice for basements, and well worth trying to track down a supplier. For more information on the Envira Cushion, call Fairway Tile and Carpet[2].

Either Comfort Base or Envira Cushion will make your tootsies a lot warmer, especially during the winter.

Laying carpet in a basement is slightly different than laying carpet on a regular floor. Here's how to go about the project.

1. Clean and seal the concrete floor.

2. Glue down the Comfort Base or Envira Cushion to the cement or wooden sub floor with a builders adhesive like PL -200 by Franklin. Leave room for a 3" wooden strip around the entire circumference of the area that will be carpeted.

3. Take 1" x 3"s and rip them down to 3/4 inch in height, so that your strips are 3 inches wide and 3/4" thick.

4. Frame the Comfort Base or Envira Cushion with the 3/4" x 3" strips. Glue the strips down to the cement or sub floor.

---

[2] See Appendix for Supplier Phone List.

Basements

What you now have is a slab surface covered with Comfort Base or Envira Cushion "framed" with wood.

5. Lay the carpet padding on top of the Comfort Base.

   If you used Envira Cushion, you do not need padding.

6. Attach the carpeting to the wooden strip at one end of the basement and stretch the carpet.

   You now have resistance to heat loss so the floor will be warmer plus cushioning.

What Are Your Suggestions for Lighting?

The first floor joists overhead give space a plenty for all type of lighting fixtures: recessed, spot, drop, track, or fluorescent. You get the biggest bang for the buck with fluorescent.

How Should the Basement be Heated?

If you are building a recreation room, consider a direct vent fireplace. No chimney is needed and the fireplace will take the dampness out of the air as well as make the room more welcoming.

Basements

As far as regular heating is concerned, with a forced air furnace you can usually make a few minor additions to the sheet metal and without having to increase the heating plant. Be careful enclosing the furnace, make certain you keep proper ventilation. Do nothing to restrict the necessary air intake.

If there are any hot air registers in the basement, they are usually in the ceiling. That made it very easy for the contractor but is very ineffective for you. Hot air rises. Therefore you should drop a hot air register to the bottom of the outside wall in the main room. You might need to install more than one.

Also be sure to install a return air register across from the hot air register at floor level. Most builders do not install basement return air registers. In order for basement air to circulate you need to create a convection loop.

Fresh, hot air forced from a floor level heating duct rises, displacing stagnant cooler air. As the cooler air sinks to floor level it is sucked into the return air duct and returned to the furnace where it mixes with air from the rest of the house.

Basements

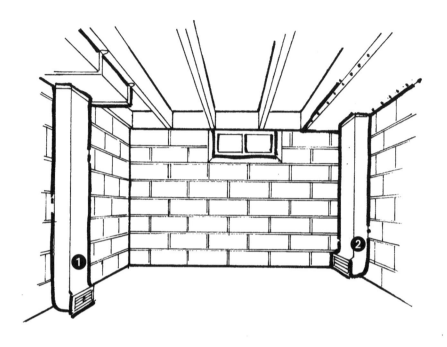

Warming and Refreshing the Air in the Basement
Dry, hot air rises. Damp, cold air sinks. To give the basement a warm, fresh, feel: 1) Drop the warm air register down to floor level; 2) Install a return air register at floor level. The warm, dry air rises to heat the entire room. The cold, damp air gets returned to the furnace.

Basements

Basement Windows

If the ground slopes away from the basement on one side, installing one or two full sized windows, or even a sliding glass door wall, opens up the basement completely and gives it a whole new look.

On the other hand, if you just have normal basement windows, consider substituting glass block if zoning permits. Building codes used to require windows that you could open and crawl through in case of fire. I defy anyone bigger than a ground squirrel to crawl though the basement windows of today.

Glass block windows give more light, and look better than standard basement windows. Glass block windows also are safer, give better insulation, and seal off a potential entryway for criminals.

When ordering glass block windows, be sure to have at least one vented window on each side of the house.

If you can't install large windows, and don't want, or can't have, glass block, consider installing magnetized interior storm windows. The interior storms will give the windows a more finished look and make the basement considerably warmer in winter.

Basements

If you are subdividing the basement into various rooms, don't forget to include fixed windows in the partitions. The glass does a great deal to open up enclosed rooms.

What About Electrical?

Basements are notoriously under lit and under powered. You'll probably want to add three or more circuits. Since it is the basement and moisture may be a problem, consider installing GFCI (Ground Fault Circuit Interrupters) outlets.

While you are making arrangements with the electrical contractor, check the memory banks. See if there are any other lights or switches that you need installed in any other part of the house. Be sure to add a surge suppresser.

Weigh the pros and cons of installing a whole house surge suppresser. The electronics in our homes are constantly getting more sophisticated and delicate. An electric power surge can destroy a great deal of equipment. Investing in a load center, surge suppresser now, may save you big money in the future. Once you get the electrician out there, it's just time. Get the most value out of his being there.

Section III
Mechanicals

Mechanicals

The Mechanicals Section is divided into chapters on Primary Heating Systems, Fireplaces, Cooling, Air Handling, and Hot Water.

I hated devoting two chapters to heating, but it is the only way to keep it simple.

Cooling is the other half of HVAC. Air Handling covers air filtration, humidification, dehumidification, air quality and air supply.

The hot water tank is that poor little thing that huddles next to the furnace in most basements. You don't realize how important it is until the water turns cold when you are in the shower.

Chapter 8
Primary
Heating Systems

Primary Heating Sources

You & Your Furnace

You folks in Southern California or Florida who consider 50° F cold may not believe this, but taken as a whole, most Americans (about 75%) have a natural gas, forced air heating system.

A few of us, especially on the East Coast, have oil and start to sweat every time somebody does something silly in the Middle East. Oil was often used when converting coal fired heating systems. It is frequently the fuel of choice on big burner systems.

Some people have propane. These poor souls are prone to cry out in anguish every time they get a heating bill. Luckily they usually live so far out in the country that the sound of their cries doesn't bother the neighbors.

Others have conventional electric. They usually live in condominiums, have special medical problems that preclude forced air systems, or purchased their home from someone who's primary concern was installation, not operation, cost.

Electric heat and in-wall natural gas heaters are also admirable choices for people who live in Southern Climes and have only an occasional use for heating. I cover your heating needs in the fireplaces and ancillary heating chap-

Primary Heating Sources

ters. You might also find the portion of this chapter devoted to Geothermal heating systems of interest. Although in your case, you may be more interested in it as a super effective cooling, rather than heating, system.

As I said, however, the majority of us rough, tough Northerners have natural gas, forced air heating systems. Over the years you've been brain-washed into believing that this is the only realistic alternative and are reasonably happy. Natural gas forced air is relatively cheap and efficient.

Like everything, it also has some negatives. Super heating air makes it desert dry. Forced air furnace blowers do a great job of circulating dust around the house. The most energy efficient models create a relatively cool and annoying draft.

You cope with this by adding humidification, trying to filter out the dust with furnace filters, and dialing up the thermostat.

Eventually, the old furnace will have to be replaced; or you will add a substantial addition or build a new home and need a new heating system. At that time, you should know that there are alternatives. Just because you, and everybody else on your block, are used to doing things a certain way, does not mean that that is the way it has to be done.

Primary Heating Sources

When considering heating system replacement, there is nothing wrong with replacing like with like, as long as you are satisfied with what you have been using. However, if you have not been satisfied, it just makes sense to weigh all the alternatives.

In this chapter we're going to look at how to determine when it's time to replace your present furnace, then look at some of the alternatives.

When to Replace?

If you have to ask, you and your heating contractor both know it's probably terminal. But how do you know when to pull the plug?

Here are a few of the tell tale signs:

1. A licensed HVAC inspector tells you that there are signs of wear on the furnace heat exchanger.

2. The furnace has to be serviced regularly during the heating season.

3. Your heating bills are going up in comparison to your neighbors.

4. The furnace seems to be running all the time trying to catch up to the thermostat setting, yet you do not feel it is warm enough.

Primary Heating Sources

When you start getting these tell tale signs, it is time to start shopping.

What to Choose?

There are heating systems today that can, at a minimum, save you 30% on your heating bills. Other systems make clean, electric heat competitive to natural gas and far more efficient than propane, while giving you an almost endless supply of hot water if you want the option.

Still others will be glad to heat your garage, and shovel the driveway and sidewalk all winter long in addition to giving you snugly heat that will keep your tootsies warm on even the coldest winter day.

Terms like Geothermal and Hydronic are forging their way into the common vocabulary of the heating marketplace. Old fashioned chimneys are out of date. They either have to have chimney liners, or are no longer necessary.

And then there's drafts. Drafts can either be completely eliminated, or so accentuated, that you get goose bumps every time the furnace goes on.

Primary Heating Sources

Forced Air Systems

Hot air systems are usually fueled by natural gas. In the country, or other places which do not have natural gas lines, these same furnaces are often adapted to use propane. Traditionally, natural gas is the most cost efficient method of heating a house. Propane and electric are much more expensive.

If you are like most of us, you presently have a natural gas, forced air heating system and you will replace it with more of the same. If your gas furnace is 20 or more years old, it may be 45 to 50% efficient, probably less. It probably started out life as a 50% efficient furnace, which meant that 50% of the heat created by the furnace went straight up the chimney, and went down hill from there.

If your furnace is 10 years of age, it may be 65% efficient, meaning 35% of the furnace heat went up the chimney without giving you a wisp of warmth. This was a big improvement over the old 50% efficient furnaces, but still was a big energy waster.

Since 1992, federal regulations have required that all gas furnaces be at least 78% efficient. The actual term is Annual Fuel Utilization Efficiency (AFUE). Over the past few years the major manufacturers have all competed to make their furnaces more and more fuel efficient, and today, many furnaces have an AFUE rating of 90% or better (or worse, depending on how you like the result).

Primary Heating Sources

Ninety percent plus furnaces have a lot going for them. Some carry AFUE ratings as high as 96%. They cost anywhere from $500 to $750 more than the 78% or 80% furnaces, but save enough on fuel bills to pay for themselves over a period of time. The colder the climate, the faster a more efficient furnace will pay for itself. Another incentive to buy a 90% plus heating system is that many power companies offer rebates when you purchase a more fuel efficient furnace.

What's the Difference Between 78%, 80%, & 90% Efficient Furnaces?

WARNING:
Many heating contractors will tell you that some of the things I am going to say in the next few paragraphs are not true. The evidence of my own senses, plus conversations with hundreds of 90%+ furnace owners tells me I am right.

Less efficient furnaces discharge air (the heat you feel coming out of the register) heated to about 125° F (warm and good feeling on a cold winter day). Air discharge temperatures in today's 90%+ models can be as low as 95° F. This lower air temperature makes the humidifier noticeably less efficient. Relatively cool dry air coming from the blower, often feels like a cold draft. Special humidifiers will make the air feel warmer.

Primary Heating Sources

Many 90%+ furnaces are louder and the furnace fan runs for a longer time. 90%+ furnaces have to be installed a little differently than older models. The increased noise factor in early models of the more efficient furnaces was often partially caused by improper installation. New designs are quieter and installation techniques have improved.

While the old, less efficient, heating plants threw a lot of heat into the house as soon as you dialed up the thermostat, the more efficient furnaces send lower heat over a longer period. This maximizes energy efficiency and cuts heating bills, but means you may stay colder, longer. You will also feel more drafts.

These problems are particularly objectionable to people over sixty. If you are older, you may want to forgo the savings and stick to a 78% or 80% efficient furnace that will give you more of the heat you are used to. Conversely, you can consign yourself to wearing a sweater all winter long and get the savings.

Reporting these negatives may make it sound like I am against 90%+ furnaces. That is not the case. I have one in my home. However, no one else talks about the drawbacks and I get a lot of negative feedback from unhappy listeners.

90%+ furnaces are direct vent models. Instead of venting exhaust up the chimney, air intake and venting is accomplished through a vent out of one of the sides of the house. Combustion air comes directly to the furnace from outside.

Primary Heating Sources

Which Furnaces Need Chimney Liners?

The 78% and 80% plus efficient furnaces still use the chimney, but require chimney liners. The reason for liners is two fold: 1- most chimneys are too large in diameter for the reduced temperature of the flue gases; 2- they are necessary to reduce temperature induced moisture buildup on the inside of the chimney that could cause an unprotected chimney to fall apart from the inside out.

How Much Should a Chimney Liner Cost?

Smart question. Pay particular attention to the cost of the chimney liner. An average price is $400 to $500 (1997 Prices) for a 35' high chimney. I have seen some replacements cost unsuspecting homeowners from $1,000 to $3,900. Any heating equipment sales person that tries to pull that kind of shenanigan, should be shown the door. Don't buy anything from him and warn your friends.

I get a lot of static from East Coast HVAC (Heating, Ventilating, Air Conditioning) contractors when I say this. They claim they can't buy a chimney liner for what I say the consumer should pay for it.

Sorry fellows. Don't pick on me, take it up with your wholesalers. There is no reason you should be paying double the rest of the country. There is also no reason why the consumer should get gouged for rigid stainless steel liner for a gas forced air furnace.

Primary Heating Sources

Conventional Electric Heat

Electricity is both a dead end and an exciting fuel of the future. Conventional electric base board heating is a very high priced alternative to natural gas. In areas where both natural gas and electric are available, natural gas may have up to 94% of the market.

The expense of electric heat means that it is usually confined to homes that are way down South, a seldom used cabin, or a room addition that cannot be effectively reached by the whole house heating system.

Bring up the name Geothermal and electricity becomes the heating source of the future. Suddenly electricity is able to compete head to head with natural gas and often come out a winner. People interested in electric heat, would be well advised to consider the Geothermal Heating system we'll describe below.

Geothermal Heating & Cooling

Geothermal heating uses mother nature to heat (and cool) your house. She also pays 40 or 50% of the heating bill. Up to four times more efficient than natural gas, Geothermal doesn't create heat. It just shifts heat from the ground to your house, or to the ground from your house, depending upon whether the system is being used to heat or cool.

Primary Heating Sources

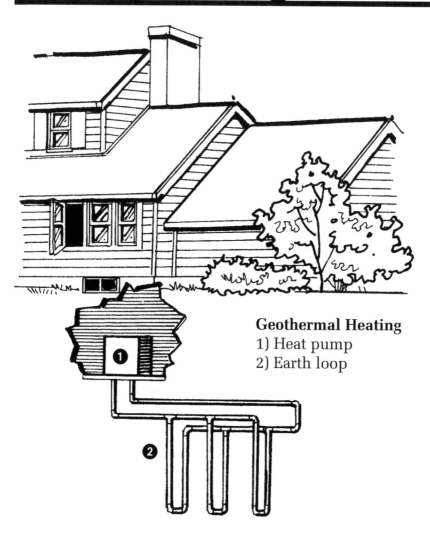

Geothermal Heating
1) Heat pump
2) Earth loop

Primary Heating Sources

The heart of the geothermal heating and cooling system is the earth loop. Loops of high strength plastic pipe are buried either horizontally, or vertically in the ground (or in a lake or pond). A heat pump is used to direct heat from, or to, the ground.

Virtually every electric power company has a Geothermal program in place at this time. Units are being installed in individual homes, condominiums, apartment and commercial complexes in Pennsylvania, Michigan, Texas and California in the U.S., all the way to Australia and Canada, internationally.

The Department of Energy likes Geothermal heating and cooling because it is efficient and restricts pollution to a single source, the electric power company, rather than a hundred million homes. This not only makes pollution easier to monitor, it cuts it down drastically.

Homeowners like Geothermal because it is cost efficient, clean, draft free. It can also save a good deal of money if you use a lot of hot water. The addition of a device called the Desuper Heater option, will provide a virtually limitless supply of hot water.

Primary Heating Sources

Boilers

Boilers heat water instead of air. They are used as replacements for heat pumps, replacement of old boiler systems, and in new construction. Residential boilers can be oil, gas, or electric powered.

The boilers of today provide the heat for water or steam heating systems. They are most commonly used with baseboard radiant heating. Hot water runs through thin copper pipes surrounded by aluminum fins, covered by the baseboard. To be effective the baseboard should run the circumference of each room.

Hydronic Heating Systems

The best description of this type of heating system is "smooth and steady all the way." Boilers combine with sub-surface (under floor) hydronic (water) heating systems to provide constant, even heat.

They are rapidly becoming the heating system of choice in many upscale new homes. The system could also be installed in a major addition that would require a new heating source.

Primary Heating Sources

Hydronic Heating

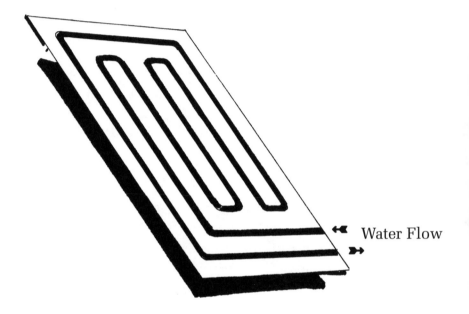

Water Flow

Hot water circulates through flooring.

Primary Heating Sources

Hydronic sub floor radiant heating systems, which use hot water circulated through piping loops under flooring, provide draft free, comfort. They completely eliminate cold spots, or rooms that remain too hot or too cool even when the rest of the house is at the preferred temperature.

A big advantage of hydronic heating is that your tootsies never get cold. Hot water continuously circulates through polybutylene tubing keeping heat constant. Because the heat is coming from the floor, maximum heat is at body level, not collecting in ceilings. Since the hot water is circulating through a sealed loop system, there is no loss of heat through holes in duct work. Manufacturers claim a savings of 20% to 40% compared to forced air.

This system can also easily heat the garage, or keep ice and snow off sidewalks and drive ways by extending a loop system under the area you wish to remain cleared before the concrete is poured.

Hydronic Heating does not use one constant loop throughout the entire house. A manifold directs different amounts of heated water to different areas. All are thermostatically controlled. If you want a specific room in the house to be ten or twenty degrees cooler than the rest of the house, so be it. If you would like just enough heat to be directed under the driveway to keep its surface at a nice ice and snow melting 33°, that is exactly what you get.

Primary Heating Sources

Sub surface hydronic heating systems can be laid under any floor surface: concrete slab, hardwood, carpeting, vinyl or ceramic tile. Since dust is not continuously blown through the house via forced air, it is far easier on who ever is in charge of the dusting.

A disadvantage of hydronic heating is that, since no ductwork is needed, air conditioning has to be an entirely separate system. If you use conventional air conditioning, a blower system and ductwork will have to be installed, significantly increasing your total equipment investment.

Combination Heat/Hot Water Systems

I am breaking this out as a separate classification because it is a separate way of looking at heating. It costs more than an ordinary forced air system, but results in an almost limitless abundance of inexpensive hot water.

Hot water tanks are very inefficient because stored water cools. Combination heating/hot water systems make a lot more hot water, faster, than conventional water heaters. Therefore less has to be stored and replacement time is shorter.

Combination heating/hot water systems are very uncommon in forced air systems, but very common in modern boiler or Geothermal systems.

Primary Heating Sources

Lennox makes a forced air unit called the Complete Heat Combination Heating System which uses a 90% Efficient natural gas furnace to heat both water in the hot water tank and a hot water coil used to heat the furnace systems forced air.

Virtually any boiler system can be used with an indirect fired domestic water heater, providing excellent water heating efficiency. As previously reported, Geothermal heating systems usually provide either hot water heating assist, or hot water heating with the Desuper water heating option.

There are a lot of heating options available today. I've got a feeling it is only going to get better. But you the buyer, the perspective new home planner, have an obligation to learn all you can, before you choose.

What is the best heating system?
Which is the best furnace?

Some combination of these two questions has to rank among my ten most asked questions. I give the same answer every time. The best furnace is the one that is installed correctly. That is also the best heating system.

Primary Heating Sources

If you choose a natural gas or propane forced air heating system, you should know that although there are hundreds of different name plates around the country, there are only a handful of furnace manufacturers. This handful of manufacturers would not be one of the survivors if they did not make pretty good equipment.

The most important person in the loop is the installation contractor. The company that is selling, installing, and will service your furnace. You don't write a check to a furnace manufacturer. You write it to the installing contractor. You won't call the manufacturer at 4 a.m. on a cold winter morning when your furnace just quit. You call the installing contractor.

Choose the correct contractor and you will have an excellent furnace no matter what the brand. Choose a bad contractor and you will have nothing but problems no matter how well the furnace was designed.

Chapter 9
Fireplaces & Gas Logs

Fireplaces & Gas Logs

Fireplaces

A fireplace can be either a decoration or an integral part of your home's heating plan. If it's just a decoration and you only want to use it once or twice a year, then anything you choose is fine.

If you actually want to use the thing, then we've got a lot to talk about. Both wood and gas fireplaces can be very efficient heat generating machines. They are certified by both the Canadian and American governments as furnaces.

Fireplaces & Gas Logs

Wood Burning

Wood burners can be tremendously efficient and very earth friendly. Wood is a renewable resource. No other type of fire is as beautiful or romantic on a cold winter's night. As far as efficiency goes, to give but one example, a Fuego wood burning fireplace delivers up to 50,000 BTU's. It is so efficient, that an entire evenings burn, will only take three or four logs. But, let's face it. You have to like splitting wood.

Pellet Stoves

Personally, I'd get gas logs, but, if you really want wood and have no room for storage, you can have the best of both worlds. It's called a pellet stove. The pellet stove is a very high tech, highly efficient heating unit.

If you are a nature lover you will love the pellet stove. It uses pellets made from paraffin impregnated sawdust that would otherwise be filling up land fills. Three or four fifty pound sacks of pellets are enough to last most people an entire winter. One pellet stove will easily throw off enough heat to keep two or three rooms toasty warm.

The one drawback to a pellet stove is that, just like a gas furnace, the controls are electric powered. If the electricity goes out, so does your fire.

Fireplaces & Gas Logs

Direct Vent - Gas

If you live in a conventional house, and want to add heating efficiency that will warm that freezing family room and a large part of the house, you cannot do better than a direct vent gas fireplace or insert by companies like Napoleon, FMI, and Heat-N-Glo.

These units are certified as furnaces and perform at about 75 to 80% efficiency. They have sealed glass fronts and combustion air comes from outside, so their is never any heat loss. Their cost usually ranges from $2,000 to $3,500.

Ventless - Gas

A ventless FMI (Fireplace Manufacturers Incorporated) gas fireplace up to 40,000 BTU's and is 99.9% energy efficient. That is more efficient than your central heating will ever be for the foreseeable future.

Fireplaces & Gas Logs

What's the Best Way to Make My Fireplace More Efficient?

If you want to upgrade a fireplace for maximum heating efficiency, consider a zero clearance, direct vent, fireplace insert. If you will just use it occasionally, get gas logs.

It doesn't take a lot of cold to get me hot footing it over to the fireplace. I have always been a fan of wood fires. I still am. For my money, if you are a wood fire fanatic, there is no finer heating system than a direct vent fireplace, or fireplace insert. These fireplaces are easy to light. Their flame is magnificent, and combustion is so complete that very few ashes remain.

There is a world of difference between traditional fireplaces and factory manufactured, state of the art, fire-places. Traditional fireplaces have unrestricted air intake and unrestricted air, heat, and pollution exhaust.

Depending upon their design, the state of the art, factory built, wood burning fireplaces have limited air intake or have a sealed fire box and do not use any heat from the inside of the house. They also have a primary and secondary burn. That means that the fire gets so hot, you get a primary wood burn like you do in a traditional fireplace, and a secondary, extremely hot, gas burn.

Fireplaces & Gas Logs

This secondary burn is what makes the fireplace such an efficient heat maker. It also eliminates the majority of pollutants and greatly decreases the amount of carbon monoxide produced. Because of the increased efficiency, they use about 2/3 less wood than conventional open-hearth fireplaces.

When my family and I moved into our new home several years ago, three out of four of us voted on a wood burning fireplace. It was wonderful. There is no way that you can duplicate the look and smell of burning hardwood.

Things change. Last October, my son Eric married Julie and my main man, the wood chopper, and stacker, and ash cleaner upper, moved out of the house and started chopping his own logs.

Nobody else in the family wanted the job. Barb and I huddled for about two minutes and we are now the proud possessors of, you guessed it, gas logs. Although sold as a decoration, my logs throw a heck of a lot of heat.

My family probably isn't much different from yours. Most of us no longer have a lifestyle that is conducive to savoring even the most efficient of wood fires. Wood still has to be stacked, stored, split, and brought into the house. Ashes have to be shoveled and fireplaces cleaned.

We have become more of an instant on, instant off, no maintenance please, society. Over the years this has led

Fireplaces & Gas Logs

to the increasing popularity of natural gas fireplaces and logs. Today, gas fireplaces and logs by companies like Heat-N-Glo, Hunter, Napoleon, Fuego and FMI (Fireplace Manufacturers Incorporated), are so natural looking, you expect, but never have, to shovel ashes.

I'm going to talk out of both sides of my mouth for a minute. All the major manufacturers have beautiful, *natural looking*, gas logs. That means that the logs are beautiful sculptured pieces that look like partially burned hardwood logs. They even have glowing embers and a variable flame. You can buy piney wood scent to heighten the allusion.

Nothing man-made can duplicate what God does very easily. Things like that magnificent shower of sparks you get when you put a fresh log on the fire; or the ever changing kaleidoscope of shapes and colors you see when looking into a natural wood fire. Features like these, you can only expect to get from the real thing.

As a practical buyer, you have to realize that those wonderful, politically correct, thought, air, and pollution police, who run your government, are trying to stamp out your right to a wood fire.

Taking out my crystal ball, I'd say that if you want a fireplace in which you can actually burn something, gas will give you ten more years of "freedom to burn" than wood. You'll have even longer if you go electric.

Fireplaces & Gas Logs

Gas Logs

If you already have a fireplace and just want logs for ambiance seriously consider vent free gas logs. They are relatively easy to install and very economical to use.

When you install ordinary gas logs in a conventional fireplace, the damper has to be permanently set so that it is never totally closed. This means that you have heat loss up the chimney twenty-four hours a day.

This is not only wasteful, it is unsafe. When your furnace goes on, and your clothes drier is in operation, they exhaust tremendous amounts of air out of the house. Air comes in the weakest link. If you have an open fireplace flue, the weakest link is right down the chimney, potentially back-drafting smoke, carbon monoxide, and a host of other contaminants into your house.

With vent free gas logs, the damper can be closed, doing away with heat loss; yet enough air seeps through the closed damper to virtually eliminate gas smell when the burner is first lit.

I am a safety nut. With my vent free fireplace, I open the chimney flue slightly while the fireplace is in operation. According to the manufacturer's instructions, I don't have to do that. But I do.

Fireplaces & Gas Logs

When the fire is over for the night, I just press a button and the fire is out. Then I close the flue.

The family and I love it.

Time out for an important point. With today's vent-free gas fireplaces you are free to think three dimensionally. That means the fireplace does not have to be stuck in a wall and you don't need a chimney. Some manufacturers make one, two, three and four sided models. You can put the fireplace in the middle of the room, or use it as a room divider.

Companies like Jotul, one of the premier makers of fine wood stoves, also make vent-free gas stoves complete with logs, that you can use as a design element in any room of the house.

My Basement Is Cold During the Winter & Damp During the Summer. I Have a Fireplace Down There. What's the Most Efficient Way to Heat the Area?

Vent free gas logs could do an excellent job of keeping the basement toasty warm and dry all year round. Because vent free logs and fireplaces are 99.5% efficient, you can keep the chimney flue closed and no heat will be lost up the chimney.

Fireplaces & Gas Logs

If you don't already have a basement fireplace, consider a vent free gas fireplace. Installation is greatly simplified because no chimney is required. Naturally, if you're going to start using the basement more, you want to make sure you have good air circulation. Be sure to read the Basement and Air Handling chapters in this book.

Mobile Home Fireplace

For years condominium owners, and apartment and mobile home dwellers have asked me for a way to have a fireplace when no gas or wood burning installation was permissible. Until 1996, electric alternatives have never been realistic. Now a Canadian Company, Dimplex North America Limited[1], has created an electric fireplace called the Symphony.

The flame is so realistic that I was on my hands and knees looking for the fire. When you turn on the blower, it has the power to heat a room at a cost of a dime or less an hour.

The Symphony costs about $1,000, installed. But it plugs into a wall socket. When you move, you can pull out the plug and take the fireplace with you!

If you live in a very politically correct city or state, this fireplace might be a viable alternative even if you live

---

[1] See Appendix for Supplier Phone List.

Chapter 10
Cooling

Cooling

If you are shopping for air conditioning, you have to give some thought to Freon scares. Freon, that wonderful stuff that used to be the propellant in our cans of hair spray and underarm deodorant, is a principal ingredient in air conditioning.

Freon Scares

In recent years Freon scares have flared up just about as frequently as sun spots. For most of us, they will have just about as much of an impact as do sun spots.

America's Master Handyman is here to tell you to keep the faith and fear not. Central air conditioning coolant is Freon R 22. R 22 based equipment is not scheduled to go out of use until the year 2025. They will continue making R 22 based equipment until 2010.

This means that, assuming a twenty year life expectancy, the air conditioning unit you buy today, will have worn out and been replaced, before the Freon ban goes into effect (if it ever does). The replacement air conditioning unit you buy twenty years from now will be filled with another cooling agent, and you will probably never notice the difference.

I don't know if the anti Freon fad will have faded away by 2010, I do know that thirty years from now, air conditioning will be a great deal different from what it is today. Meanwhile, you'd be a lot farther ahead worrying about your kid's, or grand kid's, math scores.

Cooling

How to Shop for Air Conditioning

When it comes time to shop for air conditioning, the most important thing to check out is not the clorofloro carbons, the SEER (Seasonal Energy Efficiency Rating) rating, or even the manufacturer. Don't even bother about buying the newest of the new unless you're lonely and want a lot of service calls.

The most important part of the central air conditioning package is the person who installs, services, and stands behind the air conditioner. The air conditioning contractor is the person who is going to make you, and keep you, a happy homeowner.

All the major makers of air conditioning, Trane, Lennox, Bryant, Rheem, Carrier, Rudd, York and Heil, have regular and high efficiency units. All are, or can be, competitively priced. Since the contractor is such an important part of the process, his or her work load and the bidding procedure, do much to determine the final selling price.

When you need central air conditioning, most of your time should be spent shopping for the contractor, not the equipment. In addition to being fully satisfied about their sales and service policies, and customer satisfaction levels, you want to learn everything you can about their history with the product line.

Cooling

How long have they been in business? How long they have carried their present air conditioning line? What line did they carry before that? Why did they change?

There is a good chance the people who install your air conditioning will be the same people who installed your furnace. That's wonderful. But that doesn't mean that you don't have to check their references before you decide.

Knowing all about furnaces, doesn't mean that you know or care a lick about air conditioning. Only air conditioning references can assure you that these people know air conditioning.

Just like making a furnace purchase, you want new and old customers. Contented customers love to brag about their people. Unhappy customers should be a definite turn off. No matter how good the deal, if they aren't happy, you won't be.

Here's another tip. No one can give you a quote over the phone. Anyone who just asks how big your house is and then gives you a ball park price, should not be in business. Every house is different. To give you a proper quote the contractor or his/her representative has to come out, completely inspect the house, fill out a relatively lengthy questionnaire to determine the size, and therefore the cost of the equipment you need.

Cooling

I've listed some of the things they should check before they talk price. If they do not do these things, they are not getting enough information to give you a proper quote. If they can't do a quote right, how can you expect them to complete the job?

Information Your Air Conditioning Contractor Must Know

1. How many windows do you have? On what sides of the house are they? Do they get a great deal of exposure to the sun? Are they single pane, double pane, glass block? Are they low E glass?

2. How much sun goes through the windows? From which directions?

3. How thick are the walls? Are they insulated or uninsulated? What are their dimensions? How thick are they? What direction does each face? What are they made of?

4. What about the ceiling? How big is it? How high is it? Is it insulated? What's the R factor of the insulation? How much space is there above the ceiling? Do you have an attic? Is the space above the ceiling occupied?

5. What about the floor? Is it on ground level or above a basement?

6. What climate correction factors have to be added to the calculations?

7. How many people reside in the house? How much heat do they produce? Are they active, or inactive? At home all, most, much or little of the time?

8. How much heat do your appliances produce?

9. What about your lifestyle? Will you be in the house during the peak cooling season? Will you be at home during the day or do you really just want air conditioning for the evenings?

After the contractor or his/her representative has inspected the house and gotten the information he/she needs to answer all of these questions, very precise formulas can be used to determine the exact size and power of the air conditioning unit you require.

Cooling

Get What You Pay For

Finally, you should know generally the type of unit for which you are looking. As I wrote earlier, most of the biggies all make fine equipment. So do many of the regional, and smaller national companies. As in most things there are differences in quality. Price shoppers get low end. Quality buyers get high end if they are dealing with a reputable contractor.

Just because the contractor says he is replacing the old air conditioner with a unit that is equal to the original equipment that came with the house does not mean that you are getting quality. Builders are the greatest price shoppers of all time. In an effort to keep costs down, they often install low end units which meet only the minimum federal requirements.[1] Your home deserves better.

If you are willing to pay for quality, make sure that the extra cost gives you extra value. How does the parts and labor warranty compare to the standard? Do you get complimentary annual check ups for the first few years? How about a top of the line electronic programmable thermostat? You're doing something extra for the contractor, what is he/she doing extra for you?

---

[1] *Air Conditioning, Heating & Refrigeration News*, June 27, 1994.

Cooling

Decide what you want from air conditioning before the sales call. Air conditioners are manufactured to be able to maintain a 15° differential between the outside and the inside temperatures. On a day (or night) when the temperature is 90° F outside, the air conditioner should be able to bring the inside temperature down to 75° F. Inside temperature is measured at the thermostat, and is not level throughout the house.

On a 90° F night, the temperature on the ground floor might be 75° F, but the temperature in the upper, back bedroom, might be 85°. That might be unacceptable to you. The contractor can balance the air flow to correct the problem, but he has to know it exists, before he can correct it.

If you require specific characteristics, such as being able to cool down the upper back bedroom to 75° F, when the outside temperature is 90° F, get that performance guaranty written into the contract.

How Big Should It Be?

When getting air conditioning quotes, bigger does not necessarily mean better. You want the air conditioner to work for long periods of time to cool the house. Only when the compressor is working is the unit *conditioning* (cleaning, dehumidifying) the air. If your compressor is too powerful, the air can feel cold and clammy.

Cooling

All of today's air conditioner's list their energy efficiency rating, called a SEER Rating. The average air conditioner's SEER Rating is 10 or 11, high efficiency units are 12 - 15. The higher the SEER Rating, the higher the price. Until recently, units with a 12+ SEER Rating have been prohibitively expensive. Now, manufacturers and power companies are giving credits for the purchase of the more efficient equipment.

Check the prices on air conditioning units with SEER Rating of 10 or 11 and 12 or 12+ units. If you can get the price difference, after credits, down to the $150.00 range, go with the higher SEER Rating.

Coolers:

If you are price shopping, make certain that you are getting full air conditioning. Some low ball units treat your house like a freezing compartment and just cool, not dehumidify, the air. Cool just makes you feel clammy and can actually make you sick. The conditioning, from filtering through dehumidification, is what makes you feel on top of the world.

Cooling

Heat Pumps:

In the event that it is getting time to replace both your heating and air conditioning, and you live in the southern half of the United States look at heat pumps. A decade ago the Department of Energy and most of the Electric Companies pushed heat pumps as being the economical, environmentally benign heating and cooling solution for everyone. Naturally, they weren't. For one thing, it meant that the homeowner had to convert both heating and cooling to electricity. That usually puts a person at a great price disadvantage as compared to natural gas.

Heat pumps have improved over the years. York International introduced the Triathlon, the first natural gas heat pump, into the US market at the end of last year. If I were shopping for heating and air conditioning in the South, I would at least give heat pumps a look.

Geothermal:

Geothermal heating and cooling systems use the near constant 55° Fahrenheit temperature of old mother earth to make the house comfortable all year long. They even throw in an almost limitless supply of hot water as a free bonus. And, when the government asks for SEER Ratings, where average air conditioners have SEER Ratings of 10 or 11 and high efficiency units brag about 14 or 15, Geothermal heating and cooling systems often reach as high as 21.

Cooling

If you live in an area which has high priced natural gas, or have to heat with oil, propane or electric, Geothermal should definitely be on you shopping list. Since this heating system is environmentally benign and makes the electricity cost competitive with almost every other type of heat, the power companies are really pushing it. You may be delighted to learn about the special rate incentives your local electric utility will give you.

Naturally, not every contractor installs Geothermal systems and only an expert is qualified to talk about them. If you are interested, call your local electric utility and ask them to supply you with information and a list of qualified installers.

High Velocity System:

If you live in a house which has never had air conditioning, either because it is built on a slab, or there is no room, or because it does not have duct work, hold on, you can have air conditioning now. Actually, you could have had central air conditioning any time you wanted in the past twenty years. You just didn't know it was available to you. A product called Space-Pak® uses a series of 2" diameter insulated supply tubing emanating from the attic to air condition each room of the house.

Cooling

The Space-Pak system uses a compact exterior condensing unit, much like traditional central air conditioners, to treat the air, then disperses the cooled air from an attic mounted blower unit. This system gives very even, draftless cooling. But very few contractors even know about it. To find the nearest contractor that installs Space-Pak you will probably have to contact the manufacturer. I've listed their telephone number at the back of the book.

I Have Hydronic Heat. How Can I Get Air Conditioning?

There is no reason to hang ductwork in your house just to get air conditioning. The Space-Pak system I just mentioned will do an excellent job for your purposes. The contractor just cuts a 2" hole in the ceiling of each room and runs plastic piping from an air handler in the attic.

What Kind of Maintenance Should I Give My Air Conditioning Unit?

In depth air conditioning maintenance is not something you are qualified to do. Your central air conditioning unit should be cleaned and inspected every year.

Cooling

As a practical matter you should keep leaves, twigs and other refuse out of the condenser unit located outside your house. For the most part that means brushing them off the top. During the rag weed and pollen season, you may notice that the ragweed has sucked into the fins of the condenser unit.

When that happens, turn the air conditioning off and wash the ragweed off the fins with a gentle stream of water from the garden hose. Do not use high water pressure. The fins are very delicate and the water pressure from the hose is more than strong enough to bend them.

After you have washed down the condenser, let the unit drain completely before turning the air conditioning back on.

The Power Company Is Offering a Lower Rate for Interruptable Service. Is That A Good Idea?

My family has interruptable service and it makes sense for us. Whether or not you should have it depends upon how much use the unit is going to have and your personality profile.

Cooling

I believe the plan in most States gives the power company the right to shut down the power to the air conditioner twenty minutes out of ever hour during high demand periods. In practice, I know that my air conditioning has been off longer than that during the hottest part of summer (at least it seemed a lot longer).

If the house is empty all day and you use the air conditioning only occasionally at night, you may never use the air conditioning enough for the savings from the lower interruptable rates to pay for the plan's installation charges.

If you have a medical condition that demands the air conditioning be on, either to keep the temperature down, or to filter and dehumidify the air, interruptable service might be hazardous to your health.

For my family, and probably yours, interruptable service is fine. Most summers we hardly notice it, but I certainly do notice the savings.

Cooling

On Hot Summer Days, My Air Conditioner Is Not Up to The Job. What Do I Do about It?

Three things:

1. You may be expecting too much from your air conditioning. Your air conditioning unit does just what the name implies. It conditions air. It was never made to keep the air more than 15 ° F below the outside air. Don't expect the air conditioner to keep the temperature at 70° F when it's 103° F outside.

   Neither the air conditioner, nor your body, was made for that kind of differential. Forced into that kind of a task, the compressor will probably burn out. If it does what you ask, your body may go into shock the first time you go outside.

2. There may not be enough Freon in the air conditioner. Call the service company and tell them you want them to come out and check to see if there is enough Freon.

3. Rag weed, or other air borne contaminants, may have clogged the condenser coil. If that happens, the air conditioner becomes inefficient, the temperature goes up and the condenser works harder and harder.

Cooling

If the condenser overheats, it could burn out. Turn off the air conditioning. Let the condenser cool down. Then when it is cool, spray away the ragweed, or whatever, with your garden hose. Do not use a pressure washer. The condenser is delicate and you can ruin it with high water pressure.

After the condenser, drains and dries, turn the air-conditioning back on and see if you have solved the problem. If the problem is still there, your luck is just like mine, call the air conditioning contractor. It is time to help put his kids through college.

The House Re-Heats as Soon as The Air Conditioner Turns Off. What Is Wrong with It?

Nothing. The problem probably lies with the amount of air circulation in the attic. If your roof does not have a thermostat controlled powered mushroom vent, have one installed. It will cool down the super-heated attic and make your entire house cooler.

If you already have a thermostat controlled mushroom vent, check to see that it is functioning properly. Call your HVAC contractor and have it checked. You want both a CFM (cubic feet per minute) check and a temperature check.

It may be that the fan has worn out and not been functioning. It may not move enough cubic feet per minute to do the job, or the thermostat may be set too

Cooling

high. If it is under powered, upgrade. If the temperature is set too high, have it lowered and this should solve your problem.

Ice Forms on the Pipe Leading to the Condenser. What Should I Do?

Freezing is usually a sign of over use, or low Freon. Call the installation company and have them check, then add more Freon.

Should I Wrap the Condenser Unit in Plastic Over Winter?

That's not really necessary. Modern air conditioners are made to be self draining. They are actually better off, if you just leave them alone.

Some companies are offering special, made to fit, water proof, condenser covers. They look a lot like barbecue grill covers. The condenser's paint job will look better longer with a cover, but you really don't need it.

If you have your central air cleaned and checked every year, and do the minor maintenance I've described here, it will serve you loyally for the next twenty years. No sweat.

Cooling

Chapter 11
Air Handling

Air Handling

What Is Air Handling?

Heating and cooling could really have been part of this chapter. Both are concerned with processing air, heating or cooling it, and then sending it on its way.

We let heating and cooling stand alone, because they are such big topics. Everything else, air cleaning, humidifying, dehumidifying, freshening, delivery, even getting rid of old, used air, is taken care of in this chapter.

Let's start out with a very simple premise. This is the most important chapter in the book. If you're too hot, you can go to the mall or a movie. If you're too cold, you can put on a sweater. If the kitchen is too small, you can eat out. If the toilet doesn't work, you can go next door. Simple.

This is the chapter that talks about the air we breath. Breathing is something we do 24 hours a day. Breathing bad air is very bad business.

Any home with a forced air furnace, has ductwork. Any home with traditional central air conditioning, has ductwork. The ductwork is the circulating system, the veins and arteries of the house. It functions as the central link between the furnace and the air conditioner, and every part of the house.

Air Handling

Unfortunately, ductwork is just as ignored as your veins and arteries. You don't look at it. You don't think about it. You don't even know it's there until it stops functioning properly because you haven't given it the care it needs.

Duct Cleaning

When plaque builds up in your blood vessels, it can cause all sorts of unnice things to occur. The same thing can happen with your homes circulatory system. Only it is usually a lot easier to fix in the duct work.

When was the last time you had the ductwork inspected, tested or cleaned? If you're being honest, at least 95% of the people reading this book would have to answer "never."

Imagine how filthy your floor would be if you were living in a twenty year old house and hadn't swept the floor once in all those years. How about a fifty year old house? Or a hundred?

I'm going to let you in on a dirty little secret, the condition of your home's ductwork is even worse. When they built your house, the workmen used the ductwork as a dust pan. When the boss wasn't looking, they just swept or dumped the saw dust, cigarette butts, old sandwiches, unneeded plaster, old newspapers, beer bottles (yes, beer bottles) and whatever else they wanted to get rid of into the unprotected ductwork openings.

Air Handling

You've been breathing this stuff every time your furnace blower motor goes on for the last five, ten, twenty, fifty years. Is it any wonder you get a sinus condition during the winter?

If you haven't had the ductwork in your home cleaned at least every five or six years, I strongly recommend that you have your furnace cleaned, now.

In many States there are a lot of also rans in the duct cleaning business. By calling the National Air Duct Cleaners Association[1] you can get the names and telephone numbers of the serious professionals near you. If you ask for the names and phone numbers of the Certified Duct Cleaners in your State, you'll get the information you need to select the best of the best.

I'll write more about it in *Fix It Fast and Easy 3, Frantic Fixes*, (sorry I don't have enough room here) but if you would like to learn what potentially dangerous microorganisms are living in your ductwork, you can call Connie Morbach at Sanit Air[2] and arrange to have them send you a microbial test kit. For under fifty dollars they will send you a culture kit that you attach to the air register, then return to them. When Sanit Air gets it, they grow the culture, test it, and report the results back to you.

---

[1] See Appendix for Supplier Phone List.
[2] See Appendix for Supplier Phone List.

Air Handling

I'm telling you about this particular company because most areas in the country do not have this type of testing available. Many of those who do this testing want to charge an exorbitant amount of money. Connie, has all the advanced degrees, but keeps prices modest. When we deal with those kind of folks, we all win.

If you, or any one in your family, have severe allergies or any kind of a breathing problem, I strongly recommend this test.

Zone Heating

If you ever want proof of how wasteful we American's are, imagine this scenario. It is January 23rd. You are sitting in your favorite chair in the family room, reading Glenn Haege's magnificent book, *Fix It Fast & Easy #2 - Upgrading Your House* (this is proof that you are a good person of above average intelligence). You feel a little cool, so you get up, walk over to the hall thermostat, and turn up the heat.

Think about this for a minute. You didn't get up and put on a sweater. You got up and, by turning up the thermostat, told the furnace to increase the temperature of the entire house about five degrees. In a 2,000 square foot house, you just told the furnace to make at least 16,000 cubic feet of air, five degrees hotter.

Air Handling

The living room that has not been used in the last two years is five degrees hotter; so are the basement and the upstairs bedrooms.

There is an excellent chance that five minutes from the time you turned up the thermostat, your significant other will rush out of the kitchen and turn down the thermostat because it is getting too hot.

There has to be a better way. There is, and you don't have to put on a sweater unless you want to. It's called Zone Heating. Zone Heating controls, like the DuroZone by the Dura Dyne Corporation[3] of Farmingdale, New York, compartmentalize the ductwork.

Each Zone has its own thermostat. When you want the rooms in a particular zone heated or cooled, the damper controlling the ductwork leading to that zone is opened, letting heated or cooled air in. When the rooms in that zone are not in use, and the rooms do not have to be heated or cooled, the damper closes and no heat or cooling is wasted on those rooms.

In most cases, the entire procedure is controlled by motorized dampers in the ductwork, thermostats controlling each Zone, and a Zone control panel which tells the dampers when to open and close.

---

[3] See Appendix for Supplier Phone List.

Air Handling

A new system uses air power to open and close the dampers. The air powered system is called the TLC (Total Living Comfort) Temperature Zoning System[4] and, if available in your part of the country, sometimes costs half as much to install as traditional Zone Systems.

Let's say you divide your home into three zones. Zone 1 includes the upstairs bedrooms. During the night, you might want them 68°, but no one is in them during the day so you don't care what temperature it is.

In this case the Zone 1 damper would open at night and the thermostat would bring up the temperature in the bedrooms to 68°. When the family gets up and leaves the bedrooms at 8 a.m., the Zone 1 damper would close and no more heating or cooling would be wasted on those rooms until they were needed that night.

This does not mean that the temperature in the bedrooms would suddenly fall to 0° in the winter, or go up to 100° in the summer. The rooms will be naturally heated or cooled slightly by the ambient air temperature in the rest of the house. It's just that the bedroom's thermostat will not be trying to increase or decrease the temperature, nor force the blower to pipe heated, or cooled air to those rooms.

---

[4] See Appendix for Supplier Phone List.

Air Handling

Zone 2 might be the kitchen and dining room. You might want these rooms heated first thing in the morning and throughout the day, but after dinner no one would be in the rooms so the rooms would not have to be heated or cooled for the rest of the day.

The Zone 2 damper would open first thing in the morning and the temperature would go to your pre-selected temperature. After dinner, the damper would close and no heating or cooling would be wasted on those rooms.

Zone 3 might be the family room and living room. You might want the family room to be 70° when the kids come home from school at 4 p.m. and the room to stay that temperature until after the 11 O'clock News.

In this case the Zone 3 damper would open at 4 p.m. and let the heated or cooled air into the room. It would close at 11:30 p.m. You would be saving money by not wasting your heating or cooling dollars on these rooms any other part of the day.

Naturally, Zone Heating also eliminates the "cold room" or "hot room" phenomena. If your family room is too cold, you can turn up that zone's thermostat and make it 80° if you want to.

Likewise, if it's too hot to sleep in the back bedroom during the summer, you can shut down the cooling to every other part of the house and direct all the cooling power of the central air conditioning to the bedrooms.

Air Handling

Brrrrr! It makes me cold just thinking about it. I think I'm going to put on an extra sweater.

Air Filters

I can write all I want about the dirt and danger in your ductwork, and you will smugly assume that you don't have to worry because **your furnace has a filter**. You even changed it twice last year.

Big deal. Did you ever notice that the filter is mounted on the return air duct leading into the furnace. Its purpose is to filter out air borne materials that may be injurious to the furnace and has nothing to do with your health and welfare. After all, the manufacturer warrantees his furnace, not you.

A cheap furnace filter costs 50 or 60 cents. A the top of the line Trion[5] electronic air cleaner costs over $600. Can you reasonably believe them to do the same thing?

What's the difference? What's best? What should you buy?

There is no one answer. The place to start shopping is a needs analysis. Do you have allergies or a severe lung condition? Do you want to cut down on dust? Or do you just want your furnace to run properly?

---

[5] See Appendix for Supplier Phone List.

Air Handling

Clogged air filters are a prime cause of service calls. Dirty filters reduce the efficiency in today's high efficiency furnaces and can damage equipment.

One inch replaceable fiberglass filters are supposed to be replaced every thirty days. Many people forget and let filter replacement slip for 60 or 90 days. Then they wonder why they get stuck with a fifty buck service call.

My advice is not to bother with the inexpensive filters. The next step up is to the $4 to $6.00 range. A $5.00 filter is at least twice as effective as the fiberglass kind. Some are up to seven times more efficient. Most only have to be replaced every 90 days.

Quality features include electrostatic anti-microbial construction. Electrostatic means that in addition to the filter action, some of the filter materials develop a slight negative magnetic charge with the friction of air passage. This traps positively charged mold spores and other microscopic elements like dust is attracted to a TV screen. Webb makes one of the better ones.

Pleated replaceable filters include the Magnet 3000 and the Dust Guard High Efficiency. They are electrostatic and anti-microbial. At the top of the line of this type of filter is the 3 M Electrostatic Micro Particle Air Filter.

Air Handling

I am partial to the pleated design, and from everything that I have read, 3 M's Filtrete air filter traps a greater percentage of the extremely small microbials than any but the most expensive electronic air filters. If I had allergies or a lung condition and did not want to invest in an expensive filtering system, this is the one that I would buy.

Regular furnace air filters also come in Semi Permanent and Permanent Styles. The semi permanent styles usually have to be washed every thirty days and replaced every few years. The permanent styles also require monthly cleanings.

They may be very good, but if the filter is coarse enough to be washed, I don't have great faith that it will filter fine particles effectively. As a student of human nature, I know that the majority of people (including me), do not take proper care of high maintenance items. We just get too busy.

Besides, none of the permanent and semi permanent filters I looked at are as effective as the 3 M Electrostatic Micro Particle Air Filter at a considerably lower price. I like the idea of throwing dirt away and starting fresh with new.

You'll find all of the filters I've mentioned at one of your local home centers or hardware stores. If the one you want isn't at one store, it will probably be at the next, so keep shopping.

Air Handling

Top of the Line Electronic & Heavy Media Air Cleaners

If you're really serious about air cleaning, and anybody who gets runny noses, red, irritated eyes, or hacky coughs, yet alone someone with a serious allergy or bronchial condition, should be, you need a serious air cleaner.

When the Navy decided they had a major air quality problem in their nuclear submarines, they turned to electronic air cleaning technology developed by Trion, Inc. of Sanford, North Carolina. This technology is available to you with the Trion Max 4 and Max 5 electronic air cleaning systems.

Return air is channeled through an aluminum mesh pre filter, removing most of the larger particles, like lint, hair, skin flakes and much dust. Smaller particles become negatively charged and attracted to grounded plates located in the back of the filter.

A high percentage of the particles become stuck and stay there until washed away in the dishwasher. After cleaning, air passes through an optional charcoal filter to remove lingering odors, then goes into the furnace for heating and dispersal throughout the house through the air ducts.

Air Handling

This technology is now available from most major manufacturers. It is used in the Lennox EAC12, The Honeywell F50F, the Carrier 31KAX Electronic Cleaners. Rheem, Rudd and Comfort Air furnaces, even have a special filter speed setting, so that the air can be continuously filtered.

Unless you want to live in a bubble, this is the best air cleaning technology available. The downside is that monthly cleaning is necessary. Salesmen say that all is required is that you yank the electronic air cleaner and the aluminum filter out once a month, throw it into the dishwasher, and bam, it's all taken care of.

In practice, there are two air cleaner elements and two aluminum filters, requiring two separate wash and dry cycles. That's about two or three hours time. From a purely practical, mere man's point of view, I can't remember the last time my wife let me fool around with her dishwasher for three hours without being able to put one dirty dish in it.

Another thing. Air cleaners will no longer fit in all dishwashers. My editor's new Maytag has a column in the center of the dishwasher. We tried for a half hour to find some way to cram her electronic air cleaner unit in there and there is no way it fits. In her house, at least, the introduction of a new dishwasher consigned a six hundred dollar electronic air cleaner to the junk heap.

Air Handling

In addition to all this, there is the afore-mentioned, human factor. Kathy, my editor, and her beloved husband, never remember to change that darn thing on time. If you are like them, don't worry about it. You are not a bad person. Life is just too hectic for most people to remember to clean their air cleaner every thirty, or even every sixty days.

Once an electronic air cleaner gets corroded, it stops working. A thorough cleaning may bring it back, but until then, the air is not being filtered.

The other major method of cleaning furnace air is to send it through a thick pleated, media filter which traps air borne particles like a sponge. Once every ten months or so, the filter has to be replaced and thrown away.

This type of media filter system is available from most furnace distributors with brand names like Trion Air Bear, Research Products Corporation Space Guard, or Honeywell Media Air Filter. The cost is about 60% as much as an electronic air cleaner. In addition, you have to figure the cost of replacement filters, which can run from thirty to sixty dollars.

A lot of people ask me whether a media filter or an electronic air cleaner is better. The answer depends upon you, your lifestyle, needs, and pocket book. Price is easy. Since this is not a Do-It-Yourself project, you have to go

Air Handling

though an HVAC contractor. An electronic air cleaner should range between $550.00 and $650.00 (1997 dollars) installed. The installed cost of a media filter is about $375.00. Options and non-standard sheet metal work can increase prices.

Operating costs are minimal. Electronic systems run just a few cents a day, and use the same amount of electricity as a 40 Watt bulb. The only other cost is the hot water and detergent used cleaning the system every 30 to 60 days. Media filters cost little or nothing to run, but have to be replaced every ten months to a year.

Media filters are effective down to 1 micron in size. Electronic air cleaners are effective down to 1/10 of a micron (.1 microns). Most hay fever and allergy sufferers react to breathing in pollen, molds, spores and pet dander which are seldom smaller than six microns.

For the majority of people a 1 micron filter is effective. Smog, some dust, tobacco and cooking smoke particles are .1 micron or smaller. Viruses are too small to be filtered out by either type of air cleaner. They may get zapped by the positive electric charge.

Remember, a filter is only good when it is working. That means that to clean the air in your house 24 hours a day, 7 days a week, 365 days a year, the blower motor has to be working constantly, not just when the heating or air

Air Handling

conditioning is on. Therefore, if you want continuous cleaning, you have to buy, or your contractor has to adapt, your furnace to operate at an ultra low speed, whenever the blower is not in use heating or air conditioning.

One final caveat. If you improve the filter, or keep the blower continuously running, you are increasing the strain on the blower motor. If you have a relatively young furnace, that's fine. If you have an old furnace that wheezes every time it goes on, the increased strain could burn out the blower motor.

Air Handling

Humidifiers:

WARNING - SNOOZE ALERT
I think this is interesting and important but both my beloved wife and helpmate and ever loyal daughter fell asleep trying to read this portion. All I can tell you is that if you need a humidifier, you will find this to be fascinating. If not, it may well be a yawner.

A good, well maintained, humidifier not only makes your family, pets and house plants more comfortable, it more than pays for itself in reduced energy costs. Proper humidification allows you to dial the thermostat down and still feel warm and comfortable.

Modern humidifiers fall into two different groups. Automatic Whole House Humidifiers, which are connected to both the water line and the furnace, and Portable Humidifiers that utilize a water reservoir and are often carried from room to room.

A few short years ago Whole House Humidifiers were not available for heating systems like Electric Heat, Heat Pump, or Baseboard Hot Water. Today, led by innovative companies like Skuttle Mfg. Co. of Marietta, Ohio, there is an Automatic Whole House Humidifier for every heating system.

Air Handling

Automatic Whole House Humidifiers

Depending upon the model, Automatic Whole House Humidifiers are connected directly in the furnace, or to the warm or the cold return air plenum. All Whole House Humidifiers have one thing in common, to run most effectively their setting must be changed with temperature changes.

The type of humidifier you choose is determined by your home's heating plant. The model is determined by the size of your house. There are six distinct types of Automatic Humidifiers: Plate, Drum, Flow Through, Atomizing, Steam and Hydronic.

Plate Humidifiers

The Plate type of humidifier is old-fashioned and only used on wood or coal furnaces, in homes of 1,000 square feet or less. Rigid, water absorbing plates that look like squat letter "T"s, stand upright in a tray of water. A flow of air absorbs moisture as it passes over the moist "T" plates.

Air Handling

Drum Humidifiers

The Drum humidifier is the most popular type of humidifier in homes today. It works on the same evaporative principle as the Plate Humidifier, but because the water in the tray is absorbed into a rotating sponge drum, evaporation is far more efficient and can provide ample humidification for homes of up to 4,200 square feet.

The biggest drawbacks associated with both the Plate and Drum Humidifiers is the build up of calcium in the trays due to water evaporation during the season. The units should be cleaned by the home owner at least two or three times a season to insure efficient operation.

The Watertek®, a decalcifying humidifier filter that dramatically reduces this problem has been developed by Unique Water Filtering Technology of Sterling Heights, Michigan.

Flow Through Humidifiers

This is competitive to the Drum Humidifier. The folks at Skuttle tell me that this is the humidifier of the future. Water constantly flows over an evaporation pad and then drains out of the system. Hot air from the furnace is drawn over the wet pad and distributed throughout the house.

Air Handling

This type of humidifier can provide humidification for homes of up to 4,000 square feet. The big benefit is that since the system drains constantly, there is no calcium buildup and little maintenance is required. The drawback is that a relatively small amount of water is wasted (about $8 a year according to Research Products Corporation of Madison, Wisconsin) as it drains from the humidifier.

If you are installing a forced air furnace, the flow-through humidifier is the most efficient and easiest to maintain.

Atomizing Humidifiers

The Atomizing Humidifier System creates a fine mist of water, much of which is absorbed into air directed into the hot air system. This style is primarily designed for Fossil Fuel Furnaces, Heat Pumps and Low Temperature Heating Systems. The biggest drawback is that hard water can cause the atomizer to clog.

Steam Humidifiers

The Steam Humidifier is another special purpose humidifier. It includes its own heating element and is used primarily with Heat Pump and Electric Furnaces.

Air Handling

Hydronic Humidifiers

The Hydronic Humidifier is a real break through. It is especially designed for Baseboard Hot Water heating systems which can not use standard automatic humidifiers.

The greatest weakness of furnace humidifiers is that they require some maintenance. Depending on the mineral content in the water supply, the humidifier tray and vaporizers and evaporators may have to be treated with humidifier cleaner or tablets to wash away lime and other mineral deposits. Some manufacturers make automatic flushing timers to automatically flush reservoir-type humidifiers.

The major manufacturers of furnace mounted humidifiers are Research Products (Aprilaire), Skuttle, General Filters, and Herrmidifier.

How Can I Eliminate Sediment from Humidifier?

There are two ways that you can almost eliminate sediment. You can install a special humidifier filter that you attach in line on the small copper water line running to the filter. You should be able to find one at your local hardware store. The filter will last about two years.

Air Handling

The second alternative is to have a special flushing mechanism attached to a reservoir type humidifier, that automatically flushes most of the sediment out of the reservoir several times a day. I know that Skuttle makes this kind of attachment. If it's important to you, check availability with your installing contractor before making the final choice on which type of humidifier to buy.

RECOMMENDED INDOOR HUMIDITY LEVELS

Outdoor Temperature (Degrees Fahrenheit)	Recommended Humidity (In Percent)
+ 40^0	45%
+ 30^0	40%
+ 20^0	35%
+ 10^0	30%
+ 0^0	25%
− 10^0	20%
− 20^0	15%

The higher the outside temperature, the higher the recommended humidity.

Portable Humidifiers

Portable Humidifiers are the life savers of the humidification field. They are used when it is necessary to beef up the Automatic Humidifier, or when, for some reason, in furnace humidification is not possible.

Air Handling

If you are going to buy a portable humidifier, buy a warm air mist ultrasonic humidifier. Some of the best are made by Bemis, Bionaire, Holmes and Sunbeam. Most are inexpensive, retailing from $50.00 to $100.00.

Big console models like the top of the line Bionaire console, can cost upward of $ 500.00. This model has two huge water reservoirs, and both an activated charcoal and a HEPA air filter. It is therefore more of a whole house air purification and enhancement system, than a just humidifier.

Which ever type of humidifier you choose, set it and maintain it properly, and you will be rewarded with better health, comfort and lower heating bills.

Air Infiltration

One of the most common problems I hear about every weekend is air infiltration, permitting the house to breath. Air infiltration was not a problem twenty years ago. Houses were built loose, the fresh air required by the house and the people living in the house, was easily provided by air coming in through cracks and loosely fitted windows and doors.

As the need to conserve energy became more apparent, we tightened up the houses by caulking, sealing, adding insulation, upgrading windows and doors. All of these things, while being excellent ways to make the house more energy efficient, dramatically decrease the house's ability to breath.

Air Handling

This becomes critical during the winter when a lower than 90% efficient furnace and clothes dryer are working their darndest to "exhale" air out of the tightly sealed house, causing a partial vacuum. The result is that vital replacement air is drawn in thorough any available opening: under doors, down chimney vents, etc..

Lack of proper air infiltration has many different symptoms, all aggravating to the home owner. Steamy widows, cold walls, chimney odor, down drafts in the fireplace, long lasting cooking odors in the kitchen, mold and mildew in the bath or closets, to mention but a few.

The easiest way to solve the problem is to add a passive air replacement system, such as the Skuttle Model 216, or EqualizAir unit. A nice side benefit from your customers point of view is that adding a passive air replacement system, makes their furnace, dryer and fireplace work more efficiently.

Both the Skuttle Model 216 and the EqualizAir unit permit air to enter the house whenever air pressure is greater outside than inside the house. While both of these units are quite effective close to the furnace, they cannot be used when the exterior venting required is more than twenty feet away from the furnace. If a longer run is required, a powered unit is recommended.

Air Handling

HRV: Heat Recovery Ventilators

A good heating contractor will tell you that the Skuttle Model 216 and the EqualizAir systems have three weaknesses: 1, Since they are mechanical, not powered, they only function when there is negative air pressure. 2, In the dead of winter, when they function most, they bring in dry, frigid, air causing decreased humidity and increased strain on the furnace. 3, They only do half the job, bringing in fresh air, but not exhausting stale air.

The solution to all three of these problems is the HRV (Heat Recovery Ventilator). At its simplest, the HRV draws fresh air into the house and exhausts stale air out of the house. In the winter, the outgoing stale air heats the incoming fresh air as the two air streams pass by opposite sides of multiple layers of media inside the heat exchange core. In the summer, the air conditioned exhaust air, cools the hot incoming air.

Most companies higher end models of the HRV (sometimes called ERV for Energy Recovery Ventilator) are made with special humidity absorbing cores that humidify the dry incoming air during the winter, and dehumidify moist incoming air during the summer. Honeywell uses a desiccant-coated wheel, Broan uses an "enthalpic core" (a very ritzy name for a chemically treated Kraft medium) to transfer the water vapor.

Air Handling

Other companies, like Duro Dyne do not equip their HRV's with water vapor exchangers because they believe the vapor exchangers are too fragile, subject to decomposition from the humidity, and prone to allow some of the outgoing air to cross over to the incoming air streams.

Lennox has a really neat optional air sensor, called the Air Sentry, that continually monitors air quality and automatically increases air exchange when it detects a wide range of pollutants.

Honeywell often ties their HRV into their Perfect Climate Comfort Control System and automates the entire procedure. They also recommend exhausting the air from the kitchen, bath and utility rooms, eliminating noisy exhaust fans, and directing incoming air into the bedrooms and living areas.

An HRV system can add $800 to $1,500 or more to the cost of the furnace. A separate installation costs around $1,500. While an HRV increases the cost up front, by preheating winter air, and pre-cooling summer air, it will save money on your total energy bill at the same time it increases your home's air quality. That makes it a very good investment.

Major manufacturers of HRVs are Broan, Duro Dyne, Honeywell, and Lennox[6].

---

[6] See Appendix for Supplier Phone List.

Air Handling

How Do I Tap into the Duct Work to Heat a Cold, Damp, Basement?

Don't even think of doing that unless you get the approval of your HVAC contractor. If you just tap into the existing system, there is a good chance you could wind up ruining the air flow to the rest of the house.

The ductwork in your house is like a large soaker hose. The heated or air conditioned air fills the entire line then goes out the various ducts and heats or cools the house. It doesn't go down the little tributaries until the entire line is filled up and the air is forced into the side passages.

It sounds like it should be easy to just put in some ducts and let your furnace and air conditioner heat, dry, and cool the basement.

Unfortunately, air always takes the path of least resistance. If you indiscriminately tap into the line, you could easily lose heat in half of your house. Likewise, if you open up a return air vent a short distance from the furnace, it will take all the return air from there and leave stagnant air in the rest of the house.

Air Handling

Chapter 12
Water Heaters

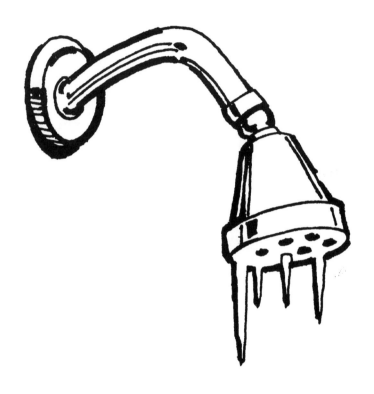

Water Heaters

It is very hard to get excited about hot water tanks. You can't impress your neighbors with them. The crème de la crème and the 1/2% homogenized versions look identical. You'd never think of saying, "Come on over to my place and check out my hot water heater."

When Should You Shop for a Hot Water Heater?

If you're lucky, the hot water heater just sits there until one day the big chill hits and you bolt out of the shower and chatter, "Hhhhoney, why dddddidn't you tttttttell me you used up all the hhhhhhot wwwwater?"

If you're not lucky, it lets go and you have the fun of dealing with a flooded basement. Many of us won't even know that the hot water heater is going to let go until we're on mop patrol.

Here are a couple hints as to when you should start shopping.

1. You are supposed to drain three gallons out of the bottom of the hot water heater every three months. If the drain water is starting to look cloudy and/or contains strong traces of rust or sediment, it may be time to give up and go shopping.

Water Heaters

2. The water does not get very hot. Most water heaters are gas fired at the bottom of the tank. Over the years rust, flaking and scaling of calcium and magnesium build-up, and sediment from water born impurities settle to the bottom of the tank, insulating the water from the heat. As the sediment builds, the heater becomes less and less efficient, while it works harder and harder to attain the desired temperature.

3. The calendar shows that the hot water tank has been in place for ten or 15 years. The life of a hot water tank is directly related to the hardness of the water. The harder the water, the shorter the tank's life expectancy. Some hot water tanks last only seven years. The average service life in a hard water area is ten years. Between ten and fifteen years is good if you are lucky enough to have soft water.

How to Test to See If the Hot Water Tank Is Operating Efficiently

1. Check to see if the water heater temperature setting is at medium. Attach a garden hose to the hot water drain.

2. Fill the laundry tub full of hot water. Don't put the stopper in until hot water is coming out. The average tub holds about 26 gallons of water.

Water Heaters

3. Test the temperature with a meat thermometer. Do not, under any circumstances put your bare hand into this water. You can get a scald burn at 114° F. The water in the laundry tub will be considerably higher.

If the hot water tank is operating efficiently, the temperature of the entire tub of water should be at least 120° F. If it is much lower, you either have the water heater set too low, or the tank is no longer heating efficiently and should be replaced. If it is much above 120° F, the setting of this high temperature should have been a conscious decision on your part. Although your washer and dish washer operate more efficiently with water at 140° F, a setting of only 120° F is the recommended industry standard for safety reasons .

What's New in Water Heaters?

In prehistoric times water heaters were armor plated cast iron affairs. Many of these monsters lasted twenty years or more. Their only weakness was rust. As the gauge of the metal grew thinner, rust became a greater problem.

Water Heaters

To solve that problem the average hot water heater of today is a steel cylinder with a thin glass lining. Technically, since the water only comes into contact with the glass lining, the water heaters should last forever. Rust is still the primary cause of failure. Now, however, the rust is often caused by water creeping through imperfections in the glass lining or at the welds that join the glass to the steel tank. It doesn't matter which way the rusting is occurring going, inside out, or outside in, rust is rust and will lead to eventual water tank failure.

The higher priced water tanks are built to combat this in three ways.

1. Better electric water heaters have a plastic inner tank. The water never gets to the metal tank so it does not rust it. Plastic tanks are possible with electric water heaters because water is heated by heating elements and the inner tank never comes into contact with direct flame.

2. State Water Heaters' State and Reliance brand's top of the line models have a patented turbo coil that swirls the incoming water at the bottom of the tank, keeping sediment in suspension. This feature means that you may never have to drain sediment from the bottom of the tank.

Water Heaters

3. Rheem/Ruud's top of the line Marathon Water heater has a front mounted flue, a miniature boiler, which heats the water outside the tank and permits the actual water tank to be of nonmetallic construction that will never rust or corrode.

Priced at around $900.00 retail, the Marathon is one of the most expensive water heaters made. The high initial price is offset by the fact that it has a lifetime limited warranty. So if you live in an area with exceptionally hard water, really object to having your water heater changed every ten or fifteen years, or just want to have the snazziest water heater on the block, it may be the way to go.

There are other water heating alternatives that have even more bells and whistles on them.

On Demand Hot Water

First of all, you can be brazen and go tankless. This will not get you arrested if you choose an on demand water heater like the AquaStar hot water system. This system produces hot water as you use it. The greater your need for hot water, the more expensive the system. Tankless systems start at about $600.00.

The smallest system, Model 80VP, only creates enough water for a home with one shower that uses a restricted flow shower head, and really has to strain to fill a washing machine or automatic dishwasher.

Water Heaters

The top of the line, Model 170VP, kicks out 165,000 BTUs and can handle most situations. I would recommend restricted shower heads if you are ever going to be using two showers at time using water from a tankless system.

Solar Power

If you live in a state like Hawaii or Arizona, you can use solar power. A solar power system often uses a non heated water tank as a collector and something like an AquaStar On Demand water heating system as a backup. Prices for these systems are quite expensive because you have the receptor tank, the solar heater and the back up system.

Lennox Complete-Heat

If you are shopping for a heating system and a hot water tank at the same time, you can go star wars and get the Lennox Complete-Heat combination heating system. Water is heated in a heating module. The hot water is used for both hot water supply and forced air heating module. According to the manufacturer it provides an almost limitless hot water supply. The heat exchanger is backed by a 15 year limited warranty.

Water Heaters

Boiler System

If you are investing in a new heating system for a new home and like a lot of hot water, you might consider a hydronic or other boiler heating system. These usually can be made to give you a limitless amount of hot water.

Geothermal

We've already talked about the limitless hot water feature that can be built into a Geothermal Heating system.

Traditional Multi Tank Systems

If you use a great deal of hot water, and want to stay with a traditional system, one of the most efficient methods of doing this is to hook two hot water tank in a series. The first tank heats the incoming cold water up to slightly above room temperature, let's say 90° F. Then, as the second tank gets depleted, when the water is being used, the relatively hot water flows into the second tank, making it much easier for the second take to heat all the water necessary to the desired temperature.

With all these choices, which is best for you? It all depends upon the hardness of the water in your area and the amount of water you need to use.

Water Heaters

Propane Water Heaters

Propane and Natural Gas Water Heaters look the same but their combustion orifices are set differently. That difference could easily kill you.

Please don't try to save money. Never use a gas water heater with propane. The heat of a propane flame is 10% hotter than natural gas and requires a different orifice. Natural gas heaters are not built to burn bottled gas safely.

A Propane fitted water heater will usually be about 10% more expensive than a similar natural gas water heater.

What Size Water Heater Do You Need?

Simple, you should buy a hot water tank based on the amount of water you use. It will also let you see how you use hot water.

Remember, the most inefficient thing you can do is store hot water. If you life style is such that you use 200 gallons of hot water in two hours, and little or none during the rest of the day, it makes sense to either change your lifestyle to a more limited method of hot water use, or invest in a hot water system that gives you the hot water you need when you demand it, but does not waste energy storing it all day.

Water Heaters

Use the form below to figure out how much water you use. Use that information to make your purchase decision.

Water Usage				
Appliance	Minimum Gal Per Minute	Maximum Gal Per Minute	Time in Minutes	Total Gallons
Bath Sink	1.5	2.5		
2 Bath Sinks	3	5		
Shower	2.5	3.5		
2 Showers	5	7		
Bath Tub	2	3		
Washing Machine	4	6		
Dishwasher	2	3		
Kitchen Sink	2.5	3		
Total Water Use				

If you like your water temperature luke warm, you probably use 50% hot water, 50% cold. If you like it hot, you could use up to 70% hot water.

The average shower takes 7 minutes. A restricted shower head could keep the water usage down to 2.7 gallons a minute. An unrestricted head can allow 3.5 gallons a minute or more. If two of you are taking hot water showers and have the washing machine going at the

Water Heaters

same time, you will be using 13 gallons a minute. In four minutes, you would use 52 gallons of water. At 70% hot water, that would amount to 36 1/2 gallons of hot water in four minutes. At that rate, it won't take you long to find yourself taking a cold shower.

How Much Should a Water Heater Cost?

The chart below will give you a good approximation of the cost of a standard electric Vs a standard gas water heater. We compare a 50-gallon electric water heater to a 40-gallon gas water heater, and an 80-gallon electric to a 50 gallon gas water heater because the slower recovery rate of an electric water heater makes a large tank essential to provide the same amount of usable hot water.

Water Heaters

Purchase Price

GAS & ELECTRIC WATER HEATERS
Cost Comparison

Type	Size	Price	STANDARD Installation	Total	Ave. Life
Electric	50 Gal	$250	$125	$375	15-20 years
	80 Gal	$425	$150	$575	15-20 years
Gas	40 Gal	$200	$125	$325	10-15 years
	50 Gal	$305	$125	$430	10-15 years

All prices are 1997 averages for comparison only. They may be higher or lower depending upon the competitive situation where you live.

Operating Expense

Heating water with natural gas is a good deal less expensive than with electricity. According to a spokesman at Consumers Power Company, a Michigan based utility that provides customers with both electricity and natural gas, operating a natural gas water heater only costs 35 to 50% of an equivalent electrically heated model.

Keep in mind that there are many occasions when electric hot water heat may be preferable to natural gas. If you have to use bottled (propane) gas, the outcome may be very different.

Water Heaters

Scald Protection

Every year thousands of people receive severe burns from their hot water supply. This is not the fault of the manufacturer. A hot water heater does what it is supposed to do. It heats water. It is up to the user to use hot water safely. Unfortunately, the very young, old, and some people with serious medical conditions cannot feel that water is scalding them until it is too late.

There is no reason for your house to be unsafe. The better faucet manufacturing companies have scald proof faucet lines. If you want to make your house safe and do not want to replace your faucets, Resource Conservation, Inc.[1] has come out with a line of ScaldSafe adapter kits for showers and faucets which will automatically shut the water off if it reaches 114° F. These kits are very economical. Call them for more information or the dealer nearest you.

---

[1] See Appendix for Supplier Phone List.

Water Heaters

Chapter 13
Plumbing
& Electrical

Plumbing & Electrical

I've combined plumbing and electrical into one chapter because they are two of the basic elements of your house that you don't even think about until something goes wrong.

This is not a "how to" chapter. There are many fine books on how to handle individual plumbing and electrical problems. For the most part, these books are excellent, profusely illustrated, and easy to understand. If you want to do major plumbing or electrical projects yourself, go to a good bookstore, a library, or the book department of your favorite home center. The purpose of my chapter is to discuss what you need to consider about upgrading in the plumbing and electrical service of your house.

Your Home's Water System:

First a brief explanation. If you have city service, water comes into your house through a water supply line under pressure that could vary from as low as 40 to as high as 160 pounds per square inch. If you have a well, it is pumped into your home under pressure. This water pressure is what gives the water the power it needs to go to every room in your house that is connected to the water supply.

Plumbing & Electrical

Incoming water travels through copper or galvanized steel pipes. An offshoot of the cold water pipe is connected to the water heater. From then on, parallel water lines, one hot, one cold, go to the various locations where they are needed.

The basic water supply travels through 3/4" pipes to the various parts of your house and to and from the hot water heater. 1/2" hot and cold water pipes are used as connections to the various locations, sink, shower, clothes washer, toilet, etc. 1/2" pipe is used as the final connection to the clothes washer, and tub/shower to enable them to fill rapidly. The sinks and toilet are connected to the 1/2" pipe by flexible 1/4 tubing.

Once the water has been used it is drained from sinks, washing machines, toilets, etc. and channeled through down sloping drains to the main drain stack, then out of your house through the sewer drain. The entire system is called the drain, waste and vent system (DWV).

Elimination of waste water and sewage is accomplished through gravitation. In other words, the water and waste goes down hill. Vent pipes interject air from the roof where-ever necessary to maintain the integrity of water seals and ease the passage of water and waste through the drain pipes.

Plumbing & Electrical

Pipes draining sinks, showers, washing machines, etc., are called *soil lines*. Pipes draining toilets are called *waste lines*. Pipes bringing in air from the vent stack are called *vent lines*.

All drains, except toilets, are connected to U-shaped pipes, called traps, which use a water barrier to prohibit noxious sewer gasses from back-drafting into the house through the drain pipe. Toilets are protected from back-drafting by the water in the bowl.

Updating the Water System

Plumbing isn't something you have to update often. Copper pipes last basically forever but they are susceptible to freezing. Unfortunately, copper pipe is connected with solder. Older solder was made with up to 50% lead. If you test the water in your home and find that it has a lead content, you may have to have the old solder taken off and the connections resoldered.

Before you do that, have the water tested twice, where it first comes into your house, and coming from the farthest faucet in the house. If the water is fine coming from the city lines, but lead contaminated when it comes out of your faucets, you probably have a solder problem.

Plumbing & Electrical

If you have to replace copper pipes or extend the lines, you may be asked if you want copper pipes or copper tubing. Tubing is better but more expensive. It is less susceptible to water hammer or freeze damage.

In a few parts of the country copper pipes are not called for in the local building code because the water is either too hard or too soft. If the water is too hard, mineral deposits build up so quickly that the copper piping becomes clogged. If it is too soft, acids in the water can attack the copper. In those areas plastic or galvanized steel pipe must be used. Galvanized steel pipe has a life expectancy of thirty-five years for hot water, fifty years for cold water.

If you have galvanized steel pipe that is about forty or fifty years old, I recommend replacing it with copper if local building codes permit.

Most houses will have cast iron drain-waste pipes. These should last for the life of the home.

PVC Pipe

I get a great many calls from listeners, about using PVC pipe. PVC pipe has a lot going for it. It is easy to install and economical. The problem is that you can only use it for cold water, even waste water over 140° F will damage it. Additionally, all plastic breaks down over a period of time (usually 50 years). If the fresh water pipe is plastic and it breaks down, the chemicals go into our drinking water.

We have hundreds of years of experience with copper pipe, barely a generation with plastic pipe. I'd prefer to err on the side of caution. I think PVC is fine for waste water drains that will never carry water over 140° F, but I'll stick with copper for my drinking water. By the way, if you have a good dishwasher, the wash and sanitizing cycles may use water as high as 160°.

Drinking & Cooking Water

When the colonists first made the trip over from Europe, they were amazed to find delightfully pure water throughout the land. We've been trying to ruin it ever since. The result has been that our water treatment plants have had a harder and harder job and had to dump in more and more chemicals in an attempt to keep us supplied with a relatively safe water supply.

Notice, I didn't say crystal clear or good tasting, I said relatively safe. For this reason the proliferation of bottled water and water filtering systems has increased dramatically. I'll write a great deal more about this in my next book, *Fix It Fast & Easy 3, Frantic Fixes*.

Plumbing & Electrical

I don't have the time or space to get into water filtration systems here. Suffice it to say, don't buy a water filtration system, until you know that you need one, or what you want to filter out of the water.

It just makes sense to have the water tested independently before you buy a filter. Never trust a water test done by a filter sales person. It was designed to show that you need to buy his product.

Your local agricultural agent will have information on where you can get water tested independently. There is a good possibility that your local land grant college even does it free.

Electrical

No major innovations in residential water supply or management have happened in the past hundred years. Most older homes don't need major upgrades of their water supply system.

It is an entirely different case with your home's electrical service. We are now living in the age of electronics. It is an entirely different world than just forty or fifty years ago. Telecommuting, the internet, home theater, and a hundred labor saving appliances we take for granted,

Plumbing & Electrical

have revolutionized electric power consumption in this country. The result is that most older home do need major upgrades in their electrical supply system.

I am certifiably friable. That means I have taken the courses, I have the certificates. I could do wiring.

I'm a fairly busy guy. When there is a plumbing problem around my house, I usually pick up a phone and call a plumber. Sometimes, because my wife will not let me forget that I Am America's Master Handyman, I get sweet talked into doing minor plumbing repairs for my family or friends (isn't it amazing how we can be strong armed into doing something for others that we wouldn't do for ourselves?).

When there is an electrical problem of any complexity, pleas from relatives, or Barbara's meaningful looks don't count. I always call a licensed electrician.

The reason for this is that with plumbing, if something goes wrong, all you get is wet. Worse case scenario, if something goes wrong while fixing the upstairs shower, or the bath starts leaking, all that will happen is that some drywall may be ruined or a few floor tiles may have popped. Not nice, but not a catastrophe.

If something goes wrong while doing electrical, you can pop yourself out of the park, blow out sensitive appli-

Plumbing & Electrical

ances throughout the house, or even start an electrical fire that smolders unseen for days, then breaks out in the middle of the night and totally destroys the house.

Upgrading the Electrical

When it comes to doing major electrical upgrades at your house, I suggest you call a professional. If you really want to get in there and DIY, you may find an electrician who is a glutton for punishment and will let you fish the wires through the studs and install some of the hook-ups.

I know that electrical is not brain surgery. I know that you can easily hook up that ceiling fan in the kitchen. The captain of the local fire department and I are proud that you upgraded all the light switches and only got shocked twice. But, when it comes to anything major, make sure a professional checks it out. All three of us will both sleep easier.

The average older home was made for a completely different power needs. Sixty amp service was the norm, most lights, two prong receptacles, and sockets, were installed in series, and most homes just had fuse boxes hidden in the basement some place.

A home today, with televisions, electric dryers, computers, garbage disposals, microwave ovens, and mega

Plumbing & Electrical

watt sound systems, needs heavy duty wiring, a 100 amp service minimum, and I would really recommend, 150 amp, 32 circuit panel, or preferably, a 200 amp, 40 circuit panel. You need grounded, 3 prong electric receptacles, with GFCIs (Ground Fault Circuit Interrupters in the kitchen and baths at a minimum. Actually, you should have circuit breakers anywhere that your could come in contact with water.

Watts, Volts & Amps

If it's been a little while since you studied about electricity in physics class, here are some basics to help you discuss electricity a little bit more easily.

Electricity is measured in watts, volts, and amps. Another word you need is ohms. Ohms is a unit of measurement for electrical resistance. One ohm equals the resistance in a circuit required for one volt to maintain a current of one ampere.

Volt is a measurement of electromotive force. Watts equals volts times amps. Amps equals volts divided by ohms. That is Ohm's law (yes, there really was an Ohm, George Simon Ohm. He was a German physicist who figured out many of these crazy calculations).

Amps stands for amperage and defines the strength of an electric circuit. So if you have a very antiquated 60

Plumbing & Electrical

amp service circuit board at your house, regardless of your requirements, only 60 amps of power should come into your house at any one time.

Just because you have a 60 amp circuit does not mean that you have 60 amps of power available for your indiscriminate use at any one time. Electric power is made available around the house via electric wires attached to individual circuits in the circuit board.

Many of the circuits are connected to a series of receptacles, or lights around the house. Quite often there will be as many as fifteen receptacles attached to a single circuit. If too many of the receptacles are being used at the same time, or if equipment demands are too high, the circuit gets overloaded and blows a fuse, or the circuit breaker snaps off, cutting power.

The wires delivering the electricity from the circuits come in different sizes depending upon the electric load they have been designed to carry. For instance, ordinary room lighting usually has a very light wire, rated at 15 amps. The circuit in the circuit box is called a 15 amp circuit.

Twenty amp circuits, attached to thicker 20 amp wires are also in the circuit box. These 20 amp circuits are designed to deliver the electric power required for small household appliances.

Plumbing & Electrical

In the case of a major appliance, or combination of appliances, let's say a big microwave, refrigerator, garbage disposer, a really powerful computer/ printer/ scanner/ monitor, or your hi-fi components, it is wise to have a dedicated circuit. A dedicated circuit is a wire that doesn't meander around the house hooked up to various receptacles, but goes directly to a particular outlet.

If you have an appliance that requires more than 20 amps of electric power, like a clothes dryer that usually requires 30 amps, or an electric range that requires 50 amps, two circuits are fused together on your circuit board and a large capacity wire cable is laid directly to the appliance.

Overloading Circuits

If your power requirements are greater than allowed by the circuit board, the fuses in the circuit board will melt and shut off the electric current until they are replaced. On more modern circuit boards, fuses are replaced by circuit breakers. When a circuit breaker is over stressed it clicks off and has to be clicked on to get electric service back.

The reason for this happening is that in physics, resistance becomes heat. If you are riding a bicycle and jam on the brakes, you smell smoke because the brakes applied resistance, which translated into heat, and burned the rubber.

Plumbing & Electrical

In an electric circuit, the more voltage going through the circuit, the greater the resistance, the greater the heat. When the heat is greater than the circuit was designed to handle, a fuse burns out on older circuit boxes or a circuit breaker turns off on newer circuit boxes.

No one likes replacing fuses or running down to the circuit box and turning on a circuit breaker. When this happens with great regularity, some people try to outwit the circuit breaker or fuse box rather than solving the problem.

It doesn't take a genius to understand that if you put a penny or a 20 watt fuse in a 15 watt fuse hole, you will be able to run from five to an unlimited amount of extra watts down the line. Doing something like that is not very smart.

Oh sure, you get the extra power, but you also build up more resistance than the copper cable was meant to handle. And, just like on the bicycle, resistance builds heat. Little by little the heat burns through the insulation. Behind the walls, the wires are running through 2 x 4's that are as dry as kindling. Sooner or later, fire happens.

If you're very lucky, you get the kids out in time. Forget the family scrapbooks and all the other possessions you've spent a life time collecting. Playing with fuses can cost you your house or your life.

Plumbing & Electrical

Minimum Power Requirements

Modern living requires a minimum of a 100 amp service for a very small house or apartment. A 1,500 or 2,000 square foot house should have at least a 150 to 200 amp service.

Don Collins, the owner of Budget Electric, an electrical contractor whose company pulls more electrical permits than any other company in Michigan, tells me that most homes do not need to be completely rewired. The old wiring can stay in place, while new, heavier wiring connects dedicated circuits required for heavier usage.

"During the summer, too many people try to run a room air conditioner off a 15 amp receptacle that is tied in with the lighting. Pretty soon the lighting is growing dim, the TV is going spotty, and they can't understand what's wrong," Don told me.

He believes that every task should have a separate circuit. That means dedicated circuits in the cooking area, at least one for the microwave, one for the electric frying pan, one for the coffee maker. You don't realize it, but an electric frying pan can use 1,200 watts of power. A microwave uses 1,200 to 1,800 watts. A coffee maker, 1,000. As a general rule, any appliance that contains a motor or a heating element, should have a dedicated circuit.

Plumbing & Electrical

If you install a central vacuum system, and I definitely recommend them, a 20 amp circuit is not enough. It should be powered with a double circuit, the same as an electric stove, dryer, or central air conditioning.

How Can I Tell If My Home Is Under Powered?

If the lights in your house flicker when a lot of power is being used, or you are burning out a good number of fuses, your wiring should be upgraded immediately. If you can't, put yourself on a power diet and stop using so much electricity.

One thing that we haven't even talked about is that if your electric system is maxed out, your appliances, lights, everything are being starved for power. Your house is providing "brown out" conditions for your appliances. When this happens electrical equipment receives insufficient power to perform effectively. Motors overheat and burn up and lights and appliances have to be replaced prematurely.

Plumbing & Electrical

What about 2 hole, Vs 3 Hole Plugs? Should Everything Be Rewired?

Prior to 1960, most receptacles were of the two hole variety. Today, all new wiring requires three hole, grounded receptacles. Generally, two hole receptacles are acceptable in bedrooms, living rooms and hallways. However, if you are going to have a rear projection TV, and lots of sound equipment, don't try to plug them into multi-receptacle 15 amp circuits and wonder why you start blowing fuses.

How Should I Set Up for Home Theater or Surround Sound?

Home theater and surround sound are the two hottest trends in home entertainment. I know that I get more enjoyment out of my big chair in the family room surrounded by speakers with a mammoth screen. I live the movies. I am in the middle of the singers. I spend a lot of time and money keeping my system state of the art.

That being said, there is no way that I can advise you on how you should wire a room for your home entertainment center until you have decided exactly what type of system you want.

For some video systems you need wires in the ceiling. Some systems need one cable, some two cables,

Plumbing & Electrical

some eight. Some require speakers to be built into the walls for optimum reproduction quality. Some do not.

The one thing I do know is that if you have the room wired correctly before the drywall goes on, you won't have to tear the walls apart and redecorate when your system is installed.

Quite often, when you are having a room addition, or any other major modernization built, you are not in a financial position to install the home theater of your dreams.

That's fine. But to get the most for your remodeling dollar you should huddle with the audio/video people who build the components you want and get a wiring layout for the system you will eventually install.

Install the wiring you will need while it only costs a little time and wire. Then, when you can afford the system, all you will have to do is hook it up. The wiring will have been done at a fraction of what it would cost later.

The One Wiring Upgrade Every Home Needs

Simple. Recently a national study of 1,000 homes was done. The homes were monitored over a one year period. The astounding result of the study was that every home received an average of about 2,000 foriegn surges a year.

Only power surges that were powerful enough to be lethal to appliances were counted. This averages approximately six to eight power surges a day. Each of these were powerful enough to burn out a garage door opener, the furnace transformer, or the delicate touch pad on an electric stove, dishwasher, television, washer or dryer.

Think of it. Your house is being subjected to 2,000 potentially lethal surges a year. At any given time your expensive equipment could be destroyed.

You do not have to put your home to this risk. All it takes to safeguard your home from most surges is the installation of a whole house surge suppresser.

The power surges are caused by the increased use of power in homes all around you. Just as your electrical usage has multiplied, so has your neighbors power consumption.

It does not have to be a bad storm, or a construction problem with the electric lines. To site just one example, if it is a hot day and most of the homes in the neighborhood have the air conditioning on. If, by coincidence, fifty or

Plumbing & Electrical

one hundred home's air conditioning goes off, a tremendous power surge will race through the lines. Your appliances are at the mercy of your neighbor's air conditioning.

A whole house surge suppresser is relatively inexpensive and can be installed easily if the electrician is already there. Just make sure he knows that you want one.

One final proviso about surge suppressers. Just because you have a whole house surge suppresser does not mean you can throw away all the individual suppressers you may have hooked up to your TV, computers, refrigerators, etc.. The individual suppressers are still needed because your appliances cause many, mini surges throughout the day. If the electric dryer turns off at the same time as the micro-wave oven, you can hit all the appliances in the house with a tremendous mini-surge.

So play it safe, protect your electric equipment investment.

Brown Out Conditions

The only other major electric problem we all share is the increased brown-out conditions during peak power consumption times. One thing you can do to help reduce the problem is to sign up for one of the restricted usage plans offered by most power companies on air conditioners and other major power users.

Plumbing & Electrical

This voluntary plan permits the power company to restrict the electric power on your air conditioner for a short period of time during peak consumption periods. You'll save money because of discounted rates, and you'll get a good feeling from being a good citizen.

The next thing you can do is to be aware during peak consumption periods. If it sounds like your equipment is laboring. Pull out the plugs on your appliances and let them wait until electric usage cools down a little bit.

Section IV
Exterior Elements

Windows, Insulation, Roofing, Siding and Walks & Drives

When we're on the outside looking in, the first things we see are the windows, siding, roofing, and concrete. Insulation, windows, roofing, and siding, are our prime protectors against the elements.

You could say this is the perfect "wrap." We're wrapping up the house and the book at the same time.

Chapter 14
Windows

Windows

Many of my most frequently asked questions are about windows. Who makes a good window? How can I get my windows repaired? How do I know when my windows have to be replaced? What type of windows should I buy? What type of storm windows are best? Why do my new windows get foggy?

A large portion of the population are living in homes with thirty, forty, even fifty year old windows. Most put up rickety storm windows every winter.

Repair Vs Replace

There are a few basic facts about windows that you should learn. As a general rule, windows are made to last about twenty years. Think of them as repairable/replaceable items just like your washer, dryer, furnace or air conditioner.

Some old, wood windows have been hanging around practically forever. They are a tribute to the maker's art. Hypothetically, you can repair these windows. I mean this literally: **You** can repair these windows.

If you think finding a good replacement window contractor is hard, try finding a contractor who is willing to come in and actually repair wood windows. The work

Windows

is very labor intensive and a window contractor can make two or three times as much replacing Vs repairing.

I know of one specialist repair company in the Detroit area (the nation's sixth largest hardware and building materials market). Most of their business is large commercial or industrial jobs. Another company, Bi Glass Systems, imports a line of epoxies from Europe which, allows them to gouge out even rotted wood and remake the window better than its original configuration. The finished product will have sealed, double glazed glass.

If you find a repair contractor, expect to pay an average of $75 to $175 per double hung window for minor repairs. This compares with average double-hung window replacement costs of between $250 and $550, depending on whether you order aluminum, vinyl, wood, vinyl clad, or fiberglass frames.

On the other hand, if you have time on your hands and the sashes are sticking, you can pull out the sashes and refinish them. By the time you are done with that, you will find that the real problem was not the sashes but the channels in which they slide, so you better replace the channels, too.

Windows

Double Hung Window

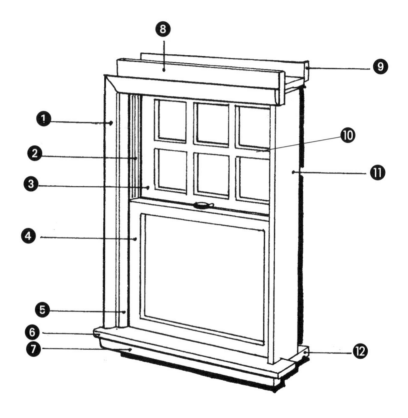

1) Inside casing; 2) Channel; 3) Upper sash; 4) Inner sash; 5) Inner stop; 6) Stool; 7) Apron; 8) Head jamb; 9) Outside casing; 10) Grill or Muntin; 11) Inside jamb; 12) Sill.

Windows

If you have a sash cord problem, you can replace the cord. Every major (read thick) How To book I know has directions on repairing and replacing sash cords. I, personally, have never replaced a sash cord, and in all my years in the business, have not met five people who actually did this type of a repair.

You can replace the sashes. Sashes are the window parts that slide up and down on a double hung window. The new, double glazed, sashes will ride up and down in the existing channels. If you have an older home, with almost irreplaceable framing, you will also save the framing.

There are two ways of looking at this. If the frames of the windows are in good condition and still square, you'll save $75 to a hundred dollars a window on materials alone, by just replacing the sashes.

Many of the larger firms, like Marvin and Caradco have created DIY friendly sash and glass kits with names like "Zap Pac" and "Tilt Pac" that make replacing a sash something you can learn to do in an hour or so. Marvin even has a step by step video. Just think of it, you can replace your drafty old windows with a state of the art wood window, for less than the cost of a vinyl.

On the other hand, if the windows are a sorry mess, maybe it's time for a complete window replacement and get an all new everything.

Windows

Buying windows is a hard nosed investment decision. Your house is probably your single biggest investment. Windows can materially effect the return on that investment.

Your house may have a wide variety of windows: fixed (no movement), single hung (only the bottom goes up and down), double hung (both upper and lower window sashes go up and down), sliding (windows slide back and forth), casement (window

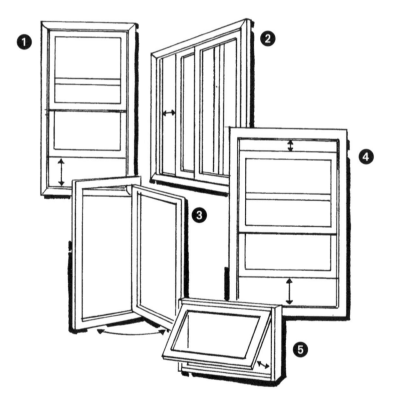

1) Single hung; 2) Sliding; 3) Casement;
4) Double hung; 5) Awning.

Windows

has hinges on one side and opens like a door), awning (window opens from the bottom), and hopper (window opens like a casement but from the bottom like an old fashioned coal hopper).

You can also have roof windows or skylights (skylights are fixed, roof windows open), sliding glass doors, and French doors.

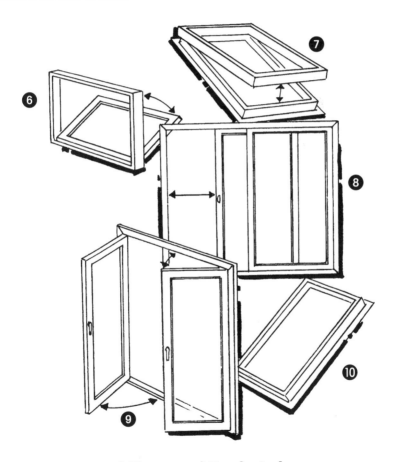

6) Hopper; 7) Roof window;
8) Sliding door wall; 9) French doors; 10) Sky light.

Windows

Window Frames

Frames can be wood, vinyl, vinyl clad, metal, composite, standard replacement, or custom made. Each has its own advantages.

It is very important to make the distinction between perception and reality. The reality is that there is really very little difference between a five dollar and a fifty dollar bottle of cologne. The perceived difference is gigantic.

The reality is that there is very little difference with the energy efficiency of a good vinyl and a good wood window. There can be a major difference in the perceived value.

Windows framed in wood, wood clad with vinyl or aluminum, or some composites are generally the most expensive. If your house was built with wood windows, it may not look as good with any other type of window framing material.

Here are some points to be aware of when considering what kind of window to buy.

- If you live in a moderately priced neighborhood, you can probably buy vinyl windows without decreasing your home's value. If you live in an upper priced neighborhood, or if your house is a beautiful older

288

Windows

cape cod, colonial, or other traditional style, vinyl windows will be an obvious new addition and could decrease the value of your investment.

- An aluminum or vinyl clad wood window combines the look of a wood window with the easy care properties of an aluminum or vinyl exterior.

- All vinyl windows are not created equal. They can vary as to insulation value of the frame, thickness of the vinyl, and the manner in which the corners are fastened together. The consensus is that welded corners are stronger than screwed corners.

- Composite windows are windows that try to do Mother Nature one better. They may have metal sheathing on the outside for protection against the elements, and vinyl sheathing on the inside for warmth, with an insulation core for protection against the elements. Andersen now has a replacement window line, called Renewal, that uses a wood/vinyl composite.

- There are hundreds of very good window manufacturers. The two most heavily advertised wood window manufacturers, Andersen and Pella, make a superior standard sized, wood clad window and have an excellent reputation with the public. However, if your windows are not the standard size, they may not be right for you.

Windows

- Miniature windows like those that every modernization salesman carries in the trunk of his car, are of no
  value unless you are buying a window for your dog
  house. Insist on seeing the real thing.
  Never buy a window without seeing the **real, full
  sized window.** This means that it is better to go to a
  showroom, rather than just have a salesman call. It
  also means that you have to see the completed job.

- The frames of high quality wood and vinyl windows
  are roughly comparable in insulation value. Wood
  has a slight edge because the frame is solid.

The frame of a composite window can have the
highest R factor (insulation value) of all. As an example,
the frame on the Hoosier St. James composite window has
outer sheathing of extruded aluminum, inner sheathing of
vinyl, and a urethane core. The core has an "R" (insulation) value 6.5 times that of wood.

Window Glazing

Window panes can be double glazed, triple glazed,
high altitude glass, Low E glass, and/or tinted glass. All
these different combinations come in both standard and
tempered glass.

The biggest insulation factor in a window is not the
frame, it is the glass. Sealed, double or triple pane, low E
(low emissivity) glass, with the air space(s) filled with an

Windows

inert gas like Argon or Krypton, is the best insulator. Marvin has a 3 pane, High R Glazing that has two Low E glass coatings, one on the inner side of the exterior glass pane, one on the outer side of the interior glass pane.

For years window salesmen have gone around bragging about the "R value" of their windows. The trouble with R values is that the number is very dependent upon whom is doing the measuring. Quality firms like Andersen, Pella, and Marvin measured the R values all around the window surface and publicized an average which gave a fair indication of the true R value of the window.

Some less conscientious companies would simply measure the R value in the center of the window where the value is highest, and publicize that as their window's R value. The result would be that the Slipshod & Shady Window Company would advertise a window with a Higher R value than the industry leaders. It wasn't true, of course, but it did sell windows.

The R value scam not only hoodwinked consumers, it drove reputable manufacturers, retailers, distributors, and contractors crazy. In an effort to establish a level playing field the National Fenestration Rating Council (NFRC) was formed.

Windows

National Fenestration Rating Council

Only a quasi governmental body could come up with a term like "fenestration." *Webster's New World Dictionary* defines fenestration as "the arrangement of windows and doors in a building."

Naturally, the NFRC has nothing to do with arranging windows and doors in buildings, but it has a great deal to do with measuring the Thermal Performance Rating or U-Factor (the amount of energy transmitted from one side of a window to the other) the Solar Heat Gain Coefficient (SHGC, the amount of solar energy penetrating a window system), the Visible Transmittance of the entire spectrum of light, and the leakage of air through the window.

You'll be glad to know that the NFRC labels on the windows of companies who have accepted this voluntary testing standard list all this information, not once, but twice, on their NFRC label. The first measurement, AA, is for residential windows of that style. The second measurement, BB, is for non-residential windows (commercial or industrial) of that style.

The idea is that every window manufacturer will eventually have a sticker on each window listing the NFRC rating. The ratings will have been done by the independent NFRC and so suddenly, like the characters in

Windows

Candide, we will find ourselves in the best of all possible worlds. Manufacturers will have a level playing field. Ma and pa homeowner will be able to compare NFRC ratings while shopping. The good will prosper. The bad, either reform or dry up and blow away.

What Does the NFRC Label Mean?

Here's what the NFRC label should show:

U-Factor: the lower the better (0.30 is better than 0.40 or 0.50).

Solar Heat Gain Coefficient: the lower the better.

Visible Transmittance: the higher the clearer.

Air Leakage: the lower the better.

If you are seriously window shopping, for around twenty-five dollars you can buy the NFRC Certified Production Directory that rates 20,000 windows. Contact the National Fenestration Rating Council[1] for details.

---

[1] See Appendix for Supplier Phone List.

Windows

Window Buying Tips.

- If you have a glaring, southern exposure, consider tinted windows for that side of the house. Tinted windows will reduce fading of carpet and, drape, chair and sofa fabrics as well.

- Vinyl windows have wider frames than wooden and aluminum windows. This means there may be noticeably less glass surface. If the window looks smaller, the frame becomes more obvious. In the worst case, this can give a "port hole" effect.

- The framing for standard replacement wooden windows usually fits inside the existing window frame. This can mean noticeably less glass surface and a larger wooden frame area. If retaining the window's original look is important, make certain that your window installer guarantees that your new windows have the same appearance and ratio of glass to window that your old windows had.

- Every year thousands of people ask me, which is the best window. The answer is very simple: the best window is the window that is installed properly. A quality installer will only work with quality materials. The "best" window, improperly installed, is worthless.

Windows

- Finding a top quality window contractor is your most important task when window shopping. Follow the rules I give on contractor selection in Chapter 1 and you will be successful. Here is a little extra advice geared specifically to windows.

1. Almost any window works for five years. When you get referrals you don't want more than one or two recent names. Ask for people who got their windows five or more years ago.

2. If you are having major window treatments installed, like bay or bow windows, make sure the referrals are for similar window treatments.

3. Start date is not important. Finish date is. Make certain that a guaranteed finish date and a penalty clause is in your contract.

4. Spell out exactly what will be done, by whom, in detail. Will the installers clean up after themselves every night? Who crates away the old window?

5. How finished will the job be when they are done? Will you be able to start hanging curtains, or will you have to install molding, paint, etc., before the job is really complete?

Windows

Is Upgrading Windows Worthwhile?

The National Association of Home Builders (NAHB) listed a comparison of metal frame, vinyl frame, and wood frame windows on their internet sight. According to this study, if you had a house heated with a moderately efficient furnace (80% efficient), and cooled with a moderately efficient air conditioner (6.5 SEER Rating), and replaced an average single glazed, metal framed window with a double glazed, vinyl framed window, you would save approximately $11.95 per year, per window.

If you replaced it with a double glazed, gas filled, Low-E glass vinyl window, you would save $13.71. If you replaced it with a doubled glazed, inert gas (like Argon) filled Low-E glass wood window, you would save $13.95.

As you can see, the biggest savings is getting a new, double glazed window. Vinyl or wood, gas filled, Low-E or not, are your options. On the other hand, many of the major window companies make Low-E glass a no cost or low cost option, so that you might as well go for the gusto and get Low-E.

Windows

Important For Do-It-Yourselfers:

1. Windows are tricky. Don't tackle a complete window installation unless you have done it before, or are a very good "finish" carpenter. Then expect it to take twice as long as you estimate it should.

2. Never measure the window yourself. There are usually no returns in the window business. If the supplier measures the window and it is wrong, he gives you a replacement at no additional cost. If you measured wrong, you are stuck paying for a worthless window.

3. Unless you are a super pro, installing a window is not a one man job. Make certain you have knowledgeable help to give you assistance. Depending on the size of the window, that person may have to hold fifty to a hundred pounds in place for a considerable length of time.

4. If you want to do it yourself, check to see if you can't get one of the sash and glass kits I wrote about at the beginning of the chapter. The sash kits only take an average of 45 minutes to install and almost anyone who is fairly handy can do it. Traditional window replacement takes hours of work and requires a high level of skill and luck.

Windows

Should I Replace Aluminum Framed Windows With Wood or Vinyl?

They still make aluminum framed windows. So if you like the windows you presently have, but just need them replaced, you can replace like with like. Metal framed windows are harder to find. Most industrial and commercial windows are metal framed. Try calling different manufacturers and distributors in larger metropolitan areas. If you want to get aluminum frames, see if you can't get thermal break windows so the frames do not transmit so much cold.

If you have to replace metal with either wood or vinyl, I would usually suggest wood from an aesthetic point of view. Metal frames are quite thin. Vinyl framed windows will be noticeably thicker.

What Are Welded Vinyl Windows?

The vinyl window industry is going to what they call a welded window. Welded window means the corners of the vinyl frames are mitered and actually melted together by precision welding.

A thicker vinyl is needed for this procedure, so the framing must be gusseted more. This procedure is a major reason window pane surface is smaller. The overall window frame is stronger, but windows can look like port holes.

Windows

What Does Low-E Glass Mean?

In Low E glass, the E stands for Emissivity, the relative ability of a surface to radiate energy compared to a black surface under the same conditions. A Low-E glass window pane has a coating on the inside that helps control the temperature of the window by changing the frequency of the light passing through it.

In the winter the window is warmer, while in the summer the window conducts less heat and is actually cooler.

Low-E glass does a couple of things. (1) It helps retard the fading affect of ultra violet rays of the sun on your carpeting and furniture. (2) It makes the window warmer, so it has a higher R value than a normal window.

Because it adds a color to the window, it also adds privacy. Just one caution: Not all Low-E coatings are the same color. Some are darker than others. Before you give the go-ahead and commit to this extra cost option, check out a life size Low-E window by that exact manufacturer and make certain that the color is not too dark for you.

Windows

Too Many Choices. Which Window Should I Choose?

The class choice is still wood or wood clad. Vinyl is becoming more and popular in lumber yards as they fight to compete with vinyl replacement window companies. Andersen's new Renewal window is an attempt to compete with a high tech composite. Another composite window company, Hoosier, makes every replacement window custom and maintains the dimensions in their master computer so that if you ever have to replace a part, they can send you the exact, made to measure, piece.

Your final choice on replacement windows may well come down to how important the interior window trim is to you. Vinyl is a relatively shiny material that comes in only a limited number of colors, usually white, beige, and brown. A special sealer is required to paint this type of surface. If you want to paint or stain the window frame inside, you have to buy a wood or wood clad window.

You have to decide which type of construction is best for your particular circumstance.

Windows

How Much Should a Window Cost?

Builders do not think nearly as poetically about your house as you do. They call a window a "hole". Grab a Midwestern contractor on a good day and ask him for a guesstimate about replacement window cost, and he'll probably tell you $400 to $600 a hole (1997 prices). Prices on the East and West Coast are higher.

No matter whether you choose a low cost vinyl, or a top of the line wood or composite window, installation cost is going to be quite similar. This means that, if you are a shrewd shopper, you might only pay a hundred dollars more for a prestige window than it's low priced cousin.

Recently (June '97), I did a spot survey of window prices at local lumberyards for my column in the *Detroit News.* I'm going to broaden and list some of the information here, not to give you pricing, but to give you a feeling for the relationship of prices between the different kinds and qualities of windows.

All of the windows in this comparison are good windows. All have double panes. All have Low E glass standard (on the Andersen) or available as a very low cost, or no cost, option. All have low conductivity spacers (the metal or plastic piece which separates and supports the two panes of glass.

Windows

All are made by extremely reputable manufacturers. All are available with complete lines, many different options and upgrades. Caradco windows, for example, can be ordered in your choice of twelve different grille options (the little pieces of wood, plastic or metal that divide windows in different designs), and sixteen different glass, insulation, and tempering options.

Vinyl windows have vinyl frames and sashes. Andersen windows are vinyl clad exterior, wood windows. Caradco and Marvin, are wood or aluminum clad exterior, wood windows (Marvin, naturally uses a heavier gauge extruded aluminum). The Saint James Hoosier Composite window has aluminum exterior, and vinyl interior surfaces, over a urethane interior core which has six times the R factor of wood.

Louisiana Pacific, Carefree, and Andersen, come in a wide assortment of standard sizes. But if you have an atypically sized window, it will have to be fitted with a smaller standard size and built out to fill the window cavity. Caradco, Marvin, and Hoosier windows can be custom made to fit your exact specifications.

I live in an automobile town, so I like to use automotive analogies. You could consider Louisiana Pacific and Carefree Vinyl replacement windows to be Fords or Chevrolets. Caradco or Louisiana Pacific wood windows could be high end Buicks or Mercuries. Andersen, Marvin, and Hoosier Composites are Lincolns and Cadillacs.

Windows

Here are some cost comparisons minus salesman's hype. Costs are for what is called a basic 32" x 24" double hung window with double pane Low E glass. It's outside dimensions would be about 3'2" wide by 4'9" tall. I've included average prices for the window only, and the window plus approximate labor. The prices are 1997 "street" (what you'd actually pay), not list prices. Like all major purchases, it pays to shop. Be on the lookout for truck load sales. During these special events you can save an honest ten percent.

1997 Street Price Comparisons

BRAND	WINDOW COST	LABOR	TOTAL
Carefree Vinyl	180	150-250	$330 - $430
Louisiana Pacific Vinyl	225	200-250	$425- $475
Caradco	250	240	$490
Louisiana Pacific Wood	235	200-250	$435- $485
Andersen Wood Clad	295	240	$535
Marvin	260-340	200-250	$460- $590
St. James Hoosier Composite	305	200-250	$505- $555

Money Saving Option for D.I.Y.'ers

As I wrote earlier, if the frames of your windows are in good shape, Louisiana Pacific (LP), Caradco and Marvin have sash only window replacement options. LP calls theirs the Smart Kit. The Caradco is called the Zap Pack. Marvin's is called the Tilt Pack. Sash only packs can cut $75 to $100 off the window price and are quite easy to install.

Windows

A handy person can do the labor him or herself. The first window should take about an hour. After that, your speed should increase to one window every 45 minutes. Think of it, you can have top-of-the-line Marvin wood replacement windows for less than the cost of vinyl.

If you feel unsure of your ability, hire an installer to put in the most difficult window with the proviso that you can help. Working with him will teach you all the tricks of the trade and you will be able to do the rest of the windows yourself and brag about the job.

Replacement Windows Are Expensive. Couldn't I Just Install New Storm Windows?

Storm windows are usually a waste of time. To be effective, they would have to provide the same type of air tight seal that you get with double and triple paned windows. That means you would have to caulk them shut. Even then, warm moist air would seep out through the interior windows and cause a condensation and freezing problem.

Interior Storm Windows

If you want to add R value, add magnetic interior storm windows. Interior storm windows are made out of acrylic sheets that are held in strips by almost invisible magnetic strips. They do not yellow, there are no hooks, no screws.

Windows

The magnetic strips provide a thermal seal that greatly reduces heat transfer and noise levels. Everyone who lives in a mobile home or on a street that has become a major thoroughfare will be amazed at the difference magnetic interior storm windows can make. They not only stop air flow, they cut noise level by almost half.

Two manufacturers of magnetic interior storm windows are **American Magnetite** and **a.1 Technologies Incorporated**[2]. Both of these companies have nation-wide dealer networks and sell Do-It-Yourself kits. Magnetite is distributed through many Sears Home Improvement Departments.

Distributors come out and tailor make the interior storms to exactly fit your windows.

Very inexpensive Do-It-Yourself interior storm windows kits are also available from the Window Saver Company[3]. The only thing not included in the kit is the acrylic sheeting which you can buy at most hardware stores.

---

[2] See Appendix for Supplier Phone List.
[3] See Appendix for Supplier Phone List.

Windows

My Single Paned Windows Are in Good Shape. Can I Reglaze Them to Make Them Energy Efficient?

A company called Bi-Glass Systems has a procedure for re-etching your existing window frames and installing double glazed windows. To give a price comparison to the window replacement study listed above. A ball park estimate for re-making the same basic 32" x 24" double hung window with double pane Low E glass, and tilt-out windows, with an outside dimension of 3'2" wide by 4'9" tall, would be about $200 to $250. The equipment would be brought out to your house, your windows taken out, re-etched, reglazed, and replaced that same day.

If you are interested, look for Bi-Glass Systems[4] in your Yellow Pages or call the home office to see if there is a dealer near you.

If there is, it would be worth while to get an estimate. You may be able to save a considerable amount of money. If there isn't, you might decide to become a licensee and make a living saving money for everyone who wants to upgrade their windows.

---

[4] See Appendix for Supplier Phone List.

Windows

I Want to Add More Light to a Room.
Will Skylights Help?

They sure will. Traditional sky lights are energy
wasters. Consider one of the new tubular roof windows
that refract light into the house. They give more light and
are far more energy efficient. There are several manufacturers, including Solatube, SunPipe and Sun Tunnel[5].
Check out your local building supply store or call the
companies for the retailers nearest you.

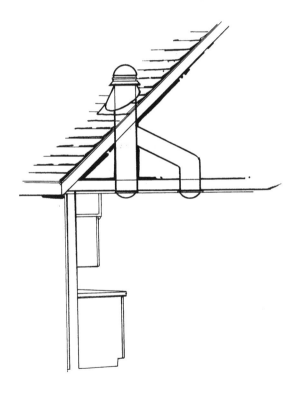

---

[5] See Appendix for Supplier Phone List.

Windows

Chapter 15
Insulation

Insulation

How Much Do You Need?

Get more.

I know that statement looks stupid, but this would be a perfectly good chapter if all I did was write those two simple words. Unless your house is only a year or so old, the probability is that it does not have enough insulation.

Insulation Theory

Remember those old movie pictures we have in of Arabian warriors riding across the desert wearing in long flowing burnooses (capes and hoods)?

During the heat of the day the burnoose kept in the perspiration and the evaporating moisture air cooled the skin. At night, when it grew terribly cold in the desert, a nomad could just roll up in his burnoose and keep warm.

Insulation is like that. It helps keep the house (and therefore you) warmer in winter, and cooler in summer. It helps seal out drafts and deaden noise. It saves you money by lowering energy bills and sometimes allows you to buy smaller, more efficient heating and air conditioning systems, which saves you even more money.

Insulation

NAHB Insulation Savings Study

How much money? The National Association of Home Builders Research Center recently did a large research study on how much a homeowner could save by making their homes more energy efficient.

With the support of the US Department of Energy and the National Renewable Energy Laboratory, they prepared a series of reports entitled: Energy Efficiency in Remodeling. The different reports covered topics like foundations, walls, roofs/ceilings, windows, ducts, water heating, and appliances. As of June 1997 these reports were available on the NAHB web site at www.nahb.com/research. You can also call the NAHB Research Center[1].

I don't have room to give you all good information available in these reports. However, they did offer charts on the potential savings available from adding certain types of insulation. I thought that starting this chapter showing the money you can keep in your pocket by adding insulation might be interesting.

The data I'm going to share with you was based on a moderate 80% AFUE (Annual Fuel Utilization Efficiency) efficient furnace and a 6.5 SEER (Seasonal Energy Efficiency Ratio) air conditioner. The tests were done in Baltimore, MD, with fuel prices of $.08 per kWh and $.55 per therm (British Thermal Energy Unit).

---

[1] See Appendix for Supplier Phone List.

Insulation

My charts are limited, there is a great deal more information in the NAHB reports.

I have edited and condensed the charts to conform to this chapter. Any error or omission is my error and has nothing to do with the good people at NAHB who provide very important technical information in copious detail.

CEILING INSULATION SAVINGS COMPARISON[2] per 100 square feet of ceiling.			
If the New Insulation Has an R Value of	And the Old Insulation Had an R Value of		
	R-8	R-15	R-19
	You Would Save		
R-19	$5.90	$1.40	
R-30	$7.80	$3.30	$1.90
R-38	$8.50	$4.00	$2.60
R-45	$8.95	$4.40	$3.30

WALL INSULATION SAVINGS COMPARISON[3] per 100 square feet of wall			
If the New Insulation Has an R Value of	And the Old Insulation Had an R Value of		
	R-0	R-7	R-11
	You Would Save		
R-11	$15.10	$2.40	
R-13	$15.85	$3.15	$0.075

---

[2] Energy Efficiency in Remodeling, Roofs and Ceilings, © 1996 NAHB Research Center, Inc.
[3] Energy Efficiency in Remodeling, Walls, © 1996 NAHB Research Center, Inc.

Insulation

BASEMENT WALL INSULATION SAVINGS COMPARISON per 100 square feet of basement wall	
Insulation Level added to uninsulated wall	Savings per 100 SF of Wall[4]
R7 Continuous, draped blanket	$12.70
R11 within 2x4 framed wall	$14.55
R11 continuous, draped blanket	$15.20
R13 within 2x4 framed wall	$15.50

What Does That Mean to Me?

I'm going to put a real simple explanation here. For the purpose of this example, let's say you had a 40' x 50', 2,000 square foot house. I'm not going to delete footage for doors and windows. The first floor has ceilings 8' high and basement ceilings 7 1/2' high. The attic has the same 2,000 square feet size as the first floor.

---

[4] Energy Efficiency in Remodeling, Foundations, © 1996 NAHB Research Center, Inc.

Insulation

Example # 1
Adding a little insulation to a badly insulated house:

If this house went from R-8 to R-19 in the ceiling, R-0 to R-11 in the walls, and insulated the formerly uninsulated basement, by going from R-0 to R-11 within the 2x4's, you'd get the following savings.

Ceiling: Going from R-8 to R-19.
20 (2000/100) x $5.90 = $118 savings per year.

Walls: Going from R 0 to R-11.
180 running feet x 8' ceiling = 1440 sq. ft.
14.4 x $15.10 = $217.44 savings per year.

Basements: Going from uninsulated to R-11 insulation applied between 2 x4 studs.
180 running feet x 7.5 ceiling = 1350 sq. ft.
13.5 x 14.55 = $196.42 savings per year.

Combined Insulation Savings: $531.86

Insulation

Example #2

Adding Insulation to a moderately insulated house
Going from moderately insulated to super insulated.

Ceilings: Going from R-19 to super insulated R-45
20 (2000/100) x $3.30 = $66 savings per year.

Walls: Going from R-7 to R-13.
14.4 x $3.5 = $ 50.40 savings per year.

Basements: Going from uninsulated to R-13 insulation
applied between 2 x4 studs.
180 running feet x 7.5 ceiling = 1350 sq. ft.
13.5 x 14.55 = $196.42 savings per year.

Total Annual Savings: $ 246.82

Insulation

Example # 3

Adding maximum recommended insulation to a badly insulated house:

If this house went from R-8 to R-38 (Recommended) in the ceiling, R-0 to R-13 (Recommended) in the walls, and insulated the formerly uninsulated basement, by going from R-0 to R-13n (Recommended) within the 2x4 s, you'd get the following savings.

Ceiling: Going from R-8 to R-38.
20 (2000/100) x $8.50 = $170 savings per year.

Walls: Going from R 0 to R-13.
180 running feet x 8' ceiling = 1440 sq. ft.
14.4 x $15.85 = $228.24 savings per year.

Basements: Going from uninsulated to R-13 insulation applied between 2 x4 studs.
180 running feet x 7.5 ceiling = 1350 sq. ft.
13.5 x 15.85 = $213.98 savings per year.

Total Annual Savings: $ 612.22

Insulation

Pretty Impressive Savings! But How Do I Get Them?

Insulating Materials:

First you have to decide which type of insulation to buy, for what reasons.

Here's a brief run down on the various types of insulation and what they are usually used for.

Formed Fiberglass

Fiberglass comes in batts, blankets, and loose. Some batts are backed with kraft paper or foil to act as vapor barriers. Some are encapsulated in porous plastic bags. According to a report by the National Association of Home Builders, fiberglass batt insulation has an R-factor of from 3.1 to 4.3 per inch.

Fiberglass batts are used for insulating attics and flat ceilings, cathedral ceilings, exterior walls, basement walls, floors and crawl spaces. Specialized batts are also used for sound insulation between walls.

Batts are just wide enough to fit between the joists. Their size is classified by their R Value. Not all thicknesses of the same manufacturers fiberglass has the same R-Value. For instance, glancing at Owens Corning's cata-

Insulation

log, I saw that their R-11 Batt is 3 1/2" thick and provides R-11 in insulation value. This particular batt is primarily used for insulating basement walls. They also have an R-13 Batt, that is 3 1/2" thick, but provides R-13 in insulation value.

Similarly, Owens Corning has R-19 Batts which are 6 1/4" thick and R-21 Batts which are only 5 1/2" thick. Depending on the use for which they were designed, they also have R-30 Batts which are 8 1/4" and 9 1/2" thick.

This is not to confuse you, but only to show you that if you are buying insulation, know the exact R-value you need, the use to which it will be put, and the dimensions with which you have to work. Your home is not unique, some manufacturer has manufactured the perfect solution. You just have to be persistent enough to find it.

Batt insulation is best in attics and in new construction. It also can easily be stapled underneath the floors in crawl spaces.

Some batt insulation is made with kraft paper or foil vapor barriers. The purpose of this vapor barrier is to protect the insulation from internal, not external dampness. If you use insulation with a vapor barrier, always attach the barrier, house side in. In the attic, the vapor barrier goes underneath. In crawl space, it goes vapor barrier up.

Insulation

If you put the vapor barrier on the wrong side, the insulation will not be able to dry properly, become a breeding ground for mold, will be ruined and have to be torn out and replaced eventually.

Loose Fiberglass and Cellulose

Fiberglass and cellulose (old newspaper and wood chips), can be blown into wall cavities or on the attic floor. According to NAHB, wet spray blown insulation has an R-Factor of 3.0 to 4.0 per inch. The R-Factor of dry spray cellulose and fiberglass varies from 3.2 to 4.8 per inch.

Loose cellulose or fiberglass insulation can be blown on top of batts in an unfinished attic to increase the R Value.

This type of insulation can also be blown into the cavities inside the exterior walls, to increase their R-Factor. When insulation is blown into the walls, holes have to be made in either the interior or exterior walls.

Blown insulation is the easiest and least expensive way to add R-Value to a wall cavity.

If your house has brick or stone siding, cellulose insulation is usually preferred, because cellulose requires a smaller dimension hose and the holes can usually be hidden in the mortar line and patched so that they are almost invisible.

Insulation

If your house has aluminum, steel, vinyl, or shingle siding, pieces of the siding will have to be removed where the insulation will be blown.

The biggest enemy of loose insulation is water moisture, so make certain that if you use loose insulation, the area is dry and going to stay that way.

When you blow insulation inside a wall cavity, there are many pipes, wires, fire breaks, and 2 x 4's, which can block the insulation. Have an infrared thermography study done of your home immediately after the job has been done or deal with a company that does an infrared scan after every job to make sure that the applicator did not miss anywhere. Owners of companies that do these scans as a regular part of their installation service, tell me that they have to go back and re-do some work about 30% of the time. Imagine how often companies that do not check miss something.

All fiberglass or cellulose insulation, especially loose insulation, compacts with age. As it ages it becomes more compact, less efficient and the R-Value goes down.

Some blown insulation is blown in wet and becomes fairly rigid as it dries.

Many home centers rent loose insulation blowing equipment and will gladly sell you bags of the loose cellulose or fiberglass. I have heard that rattle snake venom is

Insulation

sometimes used in cases of severe arthritis, and I suppose if you have arthritis bad and were a real Do-It-Yourselfer, you could go to a pet store and buy your own rattle snake. I don't recommend either.

If you want to blow insulation into your attic. OK, almost anybody can do that. But please, don't try to do your own exterior walls. Blowing insulation into wall cavities is an art. You could leave your exterior walls looking like they have a severe case of acne.

Blowing insulation is usually very competitive. Why do the work yourself when someone else is willing to do the work for practically the cost of materials?

Urethane and Other Spray Foams

Urethane and other spray foams can be used to insulate cavities. According to NAHB, their R-Factors range from 3.6 to 6.2 per inch.

Foam has a lot of advantages. It is very quick and easy to use. It is very versatile. You can spray it anywhere, from sealing a hole around a water pipe, to filling a wall cavity. It is a very good insulator. Once it dries, it stays rigid. It has very good resistance to moisture.

Insulation

The problem is that it is far more expensive than batt or loose insulation. Hopefully, with increased usage, costs will go down.

If your project calls for foam, be sure you buy in commercial multi-gallon containers, not those little cans.

Foam Sheathing

Expanded polystyrene (EPS) foam sheathing has an R factor of 4.0 to 4.5 per inch. Extruded polystyrene(XPS), like Dow Styrofoam and Wallmate, has an R-Factor of 5.0 per inch. Urethane and isocyanurates sheathing has an R-Factor of 6 to 7 per inch.

Each type of sheathing is made with specific properties to solve specific problems. Some are for walls. Some for ceilings. Some for roofs. Some for basements. Some for under basement slabs. Don't mix and match them.

Foam sheathing is probably the easiest type of insulation to use. It has very good moisture resistance. Unfortunately it is also more expensive than fiberglass or cellulose.

Insulation

How Much Insulation Does My Home Need?

The more the better is a general rule of thumb. Another answer is, it depends upon whom you ask. The Council of American Building Officials issued a Model Energy Code (CABO) in 1993 that gives a fairly good recommendation for most parts of the country. BOCA, the Building Officials and Code Administrators International, has a National Building Code; and the ICBO, International Conference of Building Officials, has the Uniform Building Code. They are all different.

Your local building department will tell you the code requirements for your area.

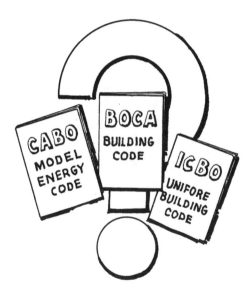

Insulation

I got permission from Johns Manville to reproduce the following CABO energy code map from their web site (WWW.johnsmanville.com). Owens Corning also has recommendations on their web site. They will give you the specifications keyed to your zip code. They are a little more conservative than the CABO standards.

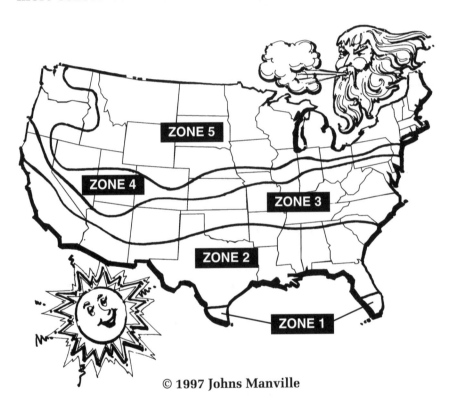

© 1997 Johns Manville

[5] Ibid.

Insulation

Typical Insulation Levels to Meet Model Energy Code Standards[6]				
Zone (Heating Degree Days)	Ceiling R-Value	Wall R-Value	Floor R-Value	Basement Wall R-Value
1 (0-500)	R-19	R-11	R-11	
2 (501-3000)	R-30	R-13	R-13	R-11
3 (3001-5000)	R-30	R-13	R-19	R-11
4 (5001-6000)	R-38	R-15	R-19	R-11
5 (6001 +)	R-38	R-21	R-19	R-15

Johns Manville recommends these levels of insulation for new construction to comply with the 1993 Model Energy Code published by the Council of American Building Officials (CABO).

In each zone, other insulation combinations can be used to comply. This recommendation assumes some construction details, including limited areas of efficient doors and windows in a typical house. Consult local building officials for code requirements in your area.

---

[6] Johns Manville Insulation Recommendations; www.johnsmanville.com/ residential/intro.html, © 1997 Johns Manville Corp.

Insulation

Insulating the Attic

Before you start, make sure you are dressed for the event. That means long sleeved shirt and pants, hard hat, gloves, goggles and respirator. What ever you are laying down, it is going to get awfully dusty. If you are working with fiberglass, it can break off and leave hundreds of little splinters in your unprotected hands and lungs. Not nice. Play it safe, not macho stupid.

It gets hotter than blazes up in the attic during the Summer. So do this in the Spring, Fall, or Winter. Don't do this in the Summer unless you have to. If you must do this in the summer, work early in the morning, and do something else during the heat of the day.

Insulating the attic is relatively fast and easy. If you have an unfinished attic all you have to do is add insulation on top of the insulation you already have. If you have fiberglass batt insulation, you can add more fiberglass batt or blow additional loose fiberglass or cellulose insulation on top of the batts. If you have loose insulation, have more blown in, do not try to put batt insulation on top of loose.

If your attic already has some insulation, it has probably settled to the point where it is only an R-7 or 8. If you're adding batts, I suggest an R-25, R-30, or R-38 batt.

Insulation

Whatever you add, make certain that you have baffles protecting the soffit vents from being plugged by the insulation. Continuous air circulation, air coming in the soffit vents and out the pot or ridge vents, is absolutely essential. If the attic can not breath, the insulation, roof deck, and shingles will be ruined. This, in turn, will cause a wet attic, eventually seeping into the plaster or drywall and degrading the home's air quality.

My Attic Is Partially Floored. What Do I Do?

You've got two answers. You could tear out the floor and just add insulation on top. This is unsatisfactory for most people who want to retain the floor for attic storage, or plan on finishing it off.

In these circumstances, it is best to lay loose or unlined insulation on the unfloored portion under the rafters, until you get to the knee wall. At the knee wall, install faced insulation, or Styrofoam up the knee wall and continue attaching the insulation on the front edges of the roof rafters. You will now have created a little "room" of insulation inside the attic.

Insulation

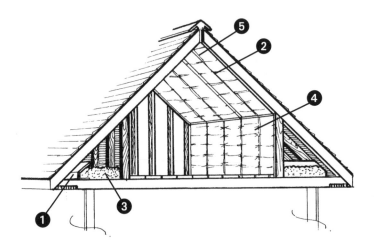

1) Soffit baffles keep insulation from plugging soffit vents.
2) Rafter vents (hidden behind insulation) provide unrestricted air flow cooling roof decking.
3) Loose or unlined batt insulation along unfloored attic at eves.
4) Lined batt insulation attached to knee walls.
5) Lined insulation going up rafters.

Insulation

Be sure to install soffit baffles to ensure air flow up from the soffit vents. It is also a good idea to install rafter vents, like Owens Corning Raft-R-Mate attic vents, between the rafters before you attach the insulation. The baffles and the rafter vents combine to assure that necessary air circulation will not be blocked.

Remember, your attic has to breath. "In" through the soffit vents. "Out" through the ridge or pot vents. This air movement cools your attic in summer and keeps your attic cold and dry in winter. (I know I keep repeating myself, but people keep forgetting. If I aggravate you enough to get you to do it right, I will have saved you a great deal of time and money.)

How Do I Insulate the Cathedral Ceiling in My Family Room?

Many insulation companies now make cathedral batts. For instance, Owens Corning's cathedral batt is 5 1/2" thick, R 25. When installing the insulation, run rafter baffles along the entire surface to be insulated. This will enable the insulation to stand off at least 1" from the roof deck boards. Always use faced insulation. Attach face side down (pointing to the living area). A ridge vent should be installed in conjunction with a cathedral ceiling design if no attic is present.

Insulation

You should also install a paddle fan in the living area. Buy a high quality six bladed model that has a computer switch.

What's the Best Way to Add Insulation to the Walls of My House?

Blown in cellulose or fiberglass. I like cellulose because it uses old newspapers and wood fiber that would usually land in the dump, to create something we need. It is a very "green" product. Good for the environment and good for the homeowner. That's a win, win combination.

Some people prefer fiberglass because it is a little more resistant to moisture and less prone to settling. All loose insulation settles over time. Rigid cellulose has eliminated most of that problem.

The choice is yours. My advice is to get a quote from both and see which you feel is best for your home.

What's the Best Way to Insulate Unheated Crawl Space?

It is very important to make certain the crawl space is well ventilated. **Do not** put a water tight vapor barrier on the ground. The ground has to breath and the area should be as dry as possible. It is best to put about two inches of gravel on the ground, then add one inch of construction quality silica sand. Blanket with Typlar or Hyplar panels and add another inch of sand.

As far as the insulation is concerned, use Styrofoam or wet foam insulation by Insta Foam to seal the cold from the floor.

How Should I Insulate the Walls of My Heated Basement?

It depends on whether you are going to attach the interior walls with furring strips or 2 x 4's. If you are going to use furring strips, insulate with Styrofoam Wallmate by Dow. The Wallmate is pre formed for the furring strips. Two inch thick Wallmate insulation panels have an R-10 R Value. That's not quite R-11, but pretty darned good.

If you are going to use 2 x 4's, you can use either Styrofoam or faced or unfaced fiberglass batts.

Shouldn't I Install a Vapor Barrier to Keep Moisture from the Insulation and Drywall?

No!!!!!!

Insulation

Good theory. Unfortunately if you install a vapor barrier, the insulation eventually gets wet and never dries. Unable to air dry, it becomes a breeding ground for mold and mildew. This not only gives the basement a nasty, musty smell, it can deteriorate to sick house syndrome.

If you install insulation and drywall or paneling without a vapor barrier, you have a 50/50 chance of having a basement leak and having to replace only the effected insulation and drywall. Replacing a few pieces of drywall is very easy to do.

If you install insulation and drywall or paneling with a vapor barrier, I guarantee that sooner or later the mold smell will have gotten so bad you will have to tear out all the insulation, ruining all of the drywall or paneling in the process.

Insulation

You Are Not Done Yet.
Sealing Out Air Leaks.

You've just spent big money on insulation. Don't forget to seal out all the air and moisture leaks you can. When you insulate, caulk and foam spray become your best friend. Sealing out wind, rain and snow keeps the insulation dry and the house warm. A good rule of thumb is: If it doesn't move, caulk or foam it.

Foam inside, then seal with caulk, every gap in your siding, windows, and weather stripping. Install new weather stripping and sweeps on all exterior doors. Caulk around dryer vents. Use foam insulation around outside spigots and pipes. Inside, caulk around window frames, seal baseboards and floor boards, insulate electrical switches and receptacles.

Down in the basement, seriously consider replacing basement windows with glass block. Glass block is a much better insulator, gives better light, and much better protection against break-ins. Install a vent in at least one glass block window on each side of the basement.

Foam and caulk all around the collar of the house where the beams are set on the concrete. Insulation here pays off big time.

Insulation

Now, Ventilate!

We've just made your house into a baggy. Everyone will be nice and warm, but not even the goldfish will be able to breath. Follow the air infiltration section at the end of chapter 14. Make certain that your home has at least a Skuttle Model 216, or an Equalize Air, better still, an HRV (Heat Recovery Ventilator).

Chapter 16
Roofing

Roofing

It's Your Turn

Sooner or later, most of us have to get our homes re-roofed. For the vast majority of us (about 90%) that means that we will have to have the shingles replaced. Of course there are other types of roofs. Some homes have tile, some slate or concrete tiles, some wood or wood look shingles, some have copper or tin.

Believe it or not, some people even have living roofs, that is the roof is formed with living sod. Those people usually only have to worry about getting their roofs mown or fertilized. If they have a bad storm or extra cold winter, they just climb up on the roof and spread some more grass seed. Unlike those fortunate few, your roof and mine won't grow back

There is a slight possibility that, if your house is presently shingled, you may choose to have the shingles torn off and replaced with slate, tile, metal or wooden shakes. Before you do, make certain that an architect or engineer has certified that your roof can take the added weight.

If you want to go the other way, from slate, tile, metal or wooden shakes to asphalt or fiberglass shingles, no problem.

Asphalt and fiberglass shingles make fifteen, twenty, twenty-five year roofs. For most of us that means that we will only have a house roofed, once or twice in our lives.

Metal, Slate, Wood Shake, & Tile Roofs

It always amazes me how many million dollar plus homes have asphalt or fiberglass shingles. Don't get me wrong. I have nothing against shingles. My house has shingles.

But, if a $600,000 a year orthodontist from Des Moines, talked himself into needing an 8,000 square foot house with two Jacuzzis and a circular Italian marble staircase leading up to who knows where, don't you think he'd want a roof that said he wasn't just one of the boys?

Metal, slate, tile, and concrete, make great statements. They reek of power and purpose. They also last fifty or a hundred years. That means that even after the orthodontist and his wife have raised their kids and moved to Costa Rica after twenty-five years, and you have bought the house, you still will probably never have to replace the roof.

Leaks are another story. Mother Nature will make certain that occasional repairs have to be made. When that happens, you can't just pull out the Yellow Pages. Your roof is a work of art. You can't trust a treasure to someone you meet on a street corner.

Roofing

Make certain that you know or learn the name of a skilled roofer who has specialized in using the materials you have on your roof for years and is willing to do repairs. If you can call down to Costa Rica and get the name of the original roofer from the retired orthodontist, do so. Otherwise, if the material is slate, you want the names of guys who work only with slate.

If you just bought the house and don't know the name of a good roofer, network. Become best buddies with your neighbors down the street who have similar roofs. Make an appointment to see a wholesaler who sells that specific type of roofing material. Ask for several recommendations.

If you don't know where to find a nearby wholesaler, go to the research section of your local library and look up the telephone numbers of the manufacturers of your type of roofing material. A call to their sales department will get you the names and phone numbers of their wholesalers.

When you start getting quotes, price is the least of your considerations. You want the guy who is absolutely the best at what he does. He is also probably the busiest. So once you've decided that this is the guy, be prepared to sit back and wait your turn.

Before you choose, you need referrals big time. Don't just drive by the referral's house. Give them a call and see if you can drop by and chat about their roofing job.

Roofing

If you have a wood shake roof (on purpose), you are a special kind of person. Only someone very special wants a roof that has to be washed and sealed like a deck. If you do it yourself, my hat is off to you. If you don't, make certain that your roofer feels that he is your best friend and offer to include him in your will. When it comes time to repair or reroof you may want to consider artificial shakes that do not burn and do not require quite as much TLC.

Flat Roofs

Flat roofs are one of the things that makes me believe Purgatory is a definite possibility. Certainly the owners of flat roofed houses must have done something very terrible in a former life. The best way to stop a flat roof from leaking is to put a gable or shed roof over it.

Enough of the one liners. If you have a flat roof and it is time to re-roof, you want me to suggest something other than moving. Although that seems to be a very reasonable alternative.

Any bituminous material you put up there is going to crack sooner or later. I suggest that you install one of the systems that utilizes an impermeable vinyl membrane. I don't believe anything is a permanent fix.

Roofing

A lifetime guarantee from a company that has only been in business five years doesn't give all that much reassurance.

If you have a builder or architect who actually recommends a flat roof on an addition that you are about to build, remember Niagara Falls. Water was meant to go down hill, not just lie there. Flat roofs sooner or later have puddles, which blossom into minor lakes, which eventually find a way of penetrating the roof's surface, flooding ceilings, light fixtures, and walls.

Shingle Roofs

Now, let's start talking about roofs for the rest of us. The shingles that cover the roofs of about 90% of the housing in North America.

If you're shingle shopping, you probably have never been the market before. Or, if you were, it was twenty years ago. The purpose of the rest of this chapter is to tell you what you need to know to become a good roofing shopper.

Roofing

Shadow Line

So what's new in shingle roofing? Not much. Shadow line, an uneven shingle height that casts a shadow and adds interest to the roof, is far more important than twenty years ago.

Solar Energy Collecting Shingles

The only other new development in roofing is the solar roof by Diversified Energy Products of Troy, Michigan (the company responsible for the power supply on solar calculators). Diversified Energy Products concept utilizes energy absorbing shingles to make the entire roof act like one vast solar panel.

This type of roofing is a great idea if you are living on a commune in the middle of the desert. My own house is hooked up to Detroit Edison and is going to stay that way. Thank you very much. They've been treating me, parents, grandparents, great grandparents, and so forth just fine, for as long as there have been electric power companies.

Roofing

Soffit Vents

If you don't need a roof that becomes a miniature power company, the next newest development is what goes under, not on top of, the roof. The big talk is about maintaining air flow through the attic.

It is perfectly legitimate to ask if this is just some Michavelian corporate strategy to increase sales. If our parents didn't need soffit vents or ridge vents, why do we? Why do we need to put this stuff on our houses now, when we didn't need them twenty years ago? Back then, as clearly as we can remember, our houses were just fine.

The answer is two-fold. First, if they knew then, what we know now, all roofs would have been made with soffit and ridge vents. Fifty years ago no one tracked the thermal dynamics of an attic in the middle of winter or summer. Air was air. A really sophisticated builder put in gable and pot vents and that was that.

Unfortunately, gable vents are usually located at, or near, the top of the roof, so the cooler incoming air just came in and went out. Gable vents also bring in air from the side, disrupting normal air flow.

Secondly, our houses have been changing. Houses used to be built loose. Fuel was cheap. There wasn't a need to put in much insulation. Just a little in the attic so the house didn't have the same thermal dynamics as the chimney and it was OK. If the homeowners didn't like the cold and drafts, they could turn up the heat, shovel in some more coal, or put another log on the fire.

Roofing

Killing with Kindness

Over a fifty year cycle, coal was replaced with electricity, oil or natural gas. Fuel prices went up. Energy conservation became a national priority. We added insulation. Windows started to be double and triple glazed and rated for R-Factor. We swathed the house in Tyvek, covered it with another layer of siding, and caulked our little fingers to the bone.

Little by little, we cut off our home's air supply. We started out with a barn and turned it into a baggy. The government loved the idea. Our roofs were not impressed.

Everybody's management book talks about "win, win" situations. In the attic it was "lose, lose" all the way.

In the winter, if we didn't add insulation to the attic, fuel bills went out of sight, and moist, hot air wafted up into the attic, where it immediately cooled, releasing moisture, rusting roofing nails, rotting deck boards, making premature roof replacement necessary. In a worst case scenarios, the water seeped down through the ceiling, ruining any plaster, drywall or insulation in its path.

On the other hand, if we added attic insulation, we saved money on heating bills but cut the air supply to the attic. This was OK during the winter because it kept the attic dry and cold. But during the summer, there was no way for the heat absorbed by the roofing to escape, and the attic became a solar steam bath baking and buckling roof boards, curling shingles, making premature roof replacement necessary.

Nice, huh?

Take a Deep Breath

The answer it turned out was ventilation. By golly, I think we may have a theme here. Throughout this entire book, to make the basement livable, we had to add air exchange. To make the living quarters healthy and comfortable, we had to add air exchange. To keep the attic from ruining the decking and roofing above, and the insulation and plaster or drywall below, we have to add, you guessed it, air exchange.

The knowledge of the indispensability of proper air exchange is what's new in roofing.

Check to See if You Have A Problem

Before I go into great depth about attic air exchange, let's see if you've got a problem. You don't have to climb on top of the roof to see if this is the year your home needs to be reroofed. Get a pair of binoculars. Go across the street and look at your roof from the neighbor's sidewalk.

Roofing

Then, go to your back fence and look from there. If the shingles look tired and worn, and much of the surface aggregate has washed away, or the shingles are rippling or curling, it's time.

Check to see how long the shingles have been down. If it is 15 or 20 years, you are due. If the shingles are 20 to 30 years old, take out your check book with a smile, you have been blessed. If the shingles are less than 15 years old, check the attic ventilation. It well may be that you are about to pay a several thousand dollar penalty for having improper attic air exchange.

If that is the case, make certain that the installation of proper soffit and ridge ventilation is part of the quote. Improper attic ventilation can cut shingle life in half and voids most manufacturer's warranties. Good attic ventilation not only extends roofing life, it can cut heating and cooling bills.

Remember what I told you in the last chapter, your attic has to breath. Breath in through the soffit vents. Breath out through the ridge or pot vents. Don't let your roofing contractor sweet talk you into just putting in ridge or pot vents. Ridge vents without soffit vents is like just only being able to exhale. It don't work that way.

Roofing

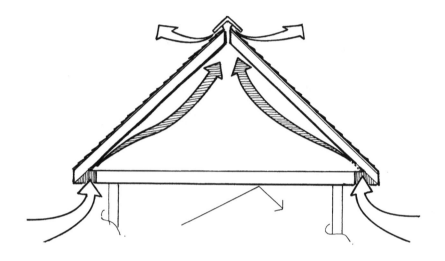

Attic Air Flow

SUMMER: Cool air comes in the soffit vents and cools the deck boards and attic. Hot air escapes through ridge or pot vents. Cool, dry, interior air stays inside, and is not lost out the attic.

WINTER: Cold air comes in through the soffit vents, warms slightly, then escapes through the ridge or pot vents, keeping deck boards cool and dry.
Relatively warm, moist, interior air, stays inside house and does not condense in the attic

Roofing

What Do I Do? The Soffits of My House Are Too Small for Soffit Vents.

If your house does not have sufficient overhang for traditional soffit vents, the problem can be taken care of by installing Combo Vents. Combo Vents have a metal top flange that creates the space necessary for venting, while providing a firm foundation for gutter installation.

More information on Combo Vents can be gotten from your roofing supplier, or by requesting information from the Combo Vent Company or Globe Building Materials, Inc.[1].

If you positively can not get Combo Vents, you can buy small round air vents at your building supply store and drill holes in the soffit. These vents are not really adequate. They are easily plugged and do not let enough air in. For air exchange to work properly in the attic, the amount of incoming and outgoing air should be equal.

Exhaust vents can be either standard roof top ventilators, or ridge vents. If you choose the roof top ventilators, you need one ventilator per 150 square feet of attic floor. Ridge vents are a great deal more inconspicuous than roof top vents. They come in several different configurations, ranging from a rigid plastic "fabric" that folds over the ridge to preformed polypropylene. Makers include Global Building Supply and the Cobra Ridge Vent by GAF Materials Corporation[2].

---

[1] See Appendix for Supplier Phone List.

[2] See Appendix for Supplier Phone List.

Roofing

Who's Going to Do The Repair?

After you discover damage the first decision is who is going to do the repairs. Are you going to do the repair or have it done by a professional? Know your limitations. Ladders are accident traps to the unwary. Roofs are one of the most dangerous places a homeowner can be. If you don't belong on a roof, don't go. The important thing is to make the decision right away. Don't procrastinate because you are intelligently concerned about climbing the ladder.

If you can't get any response, go see the people at a roofing supply company or lumber yard. Explain the problem you have to the folks at the counter and ask them to recommend a couple of people for the job.

If the repairs are minor, consider paying for an inspection and quote or ask if the repair can be done immediately so that the roofer does not have to make a call back. Insist that who ever comes out to your home to look at the roof be licensed and bring proof of insurance with him. If the repair is so large that it can not be made on the same day as the inspection, see if the area of the roof can be tarped immediately to protect your house from further water damage.

Roofing

Which Is Better, Asphalt (Organic) or Fiberglass Shingles?

Asphalt and fiberglass shingles are almost identical. Shingle manufacture begins with a base surface called a "scrim" to which all other materials are applied during the manufacturing process. When the scrim is fiberglass, the shingle is called a fiberglass shingle. When the scrim is a thick piece of felt, it is called an organic, or asphalt shingle.

Present day felt is often a recycled material composed of newsprint, corrugated and other fiber materials. Organic shingles are naturally thicker, heavier and acclimatize better to frequent changes in heat and cold cycles. Organic shingles have a Class "C" Fire Rating.

Fiberglass shingles are lighter weight, more fireproof and slightly less expensive. Fiberglass shingles have a Class "A" Fire Rating.

Most lumberyards and discount centers only carry fiberglass shingles.

Typically a fiberglass shingle will cost four to five dollars less per square than an organic shingle with a similar warranty.

Roofing

In the Great Lakes, Rockies or Pacific Northwest Areas, with their heavy snow and freezing rains, I usually recommend organic shingles. Where there is a great risk of fire, I recommend fiberglass.

In the event that you are doing the reroofing job yourself, the fact that fiberglass shingles weigh 30 to 40 pounds less per square than similar quality organic shingles, may make fiberglass a good choice.

If the roofing company has a preference between fiberglass and organic shingles, leave the choice to them. You want them to use the shingle with which they are most comfortable. The choice of quality, manufacturer, color, and dimensionality of the shingles, is up to you.

Dimensional Shingles

Dimensional shingles use ceramic or sedimentatious material to build up the thickness, is the latest advance in shingle design. It makes a dramatic change in the shadow line and gives much the same quality look as slate, ceramic or wooden shingles.

A shingle's color and shadow line is important because it can have a great impact on the sales appeal of your home. Many home buyers make their gut purchase decision as they drive up to the house and get out of the car. What they see first (curb appeal), can make or break, the sale.

Roofing

On a single story house, roof shingles, their color and shadow line, make the largest visual impression of any aspect of the house. Shadow line is not as critical on a two or three story house, because prospects can not see as much of the roof from ground level.

Casing the Neighborhood

Before you buy shingles, drive around your neighborhood. See what color and shadow line the other houses have, especially the newer homes and those that have been recently re-shingled. If many of the home owners have upgraded to the new raised pattern shingles, it may be smart for you to do the same.

After you've checked out the neighborhood, go to a wholesale roofing supply to look at the styles, quality and color selections available. These people supply professionals, they have major displays and a great deal of product information. Give them a call first, tell them that you are getting your house reroofed. Ask when would be a good time to stop by.

After you've gotten a good grounding on shingles, get their recommendation on roofing contractors. The roofing wholesaler knows who has been building a good business year after year. When the wholesaler gives you the name of two or three roofing contractors, they are people in whom he has confidence.

Roofing

Other good places to get information and recommendations are the contract departments at your local building materials discounter, home center and lumber yard. If a friend or relative has recently had a roofing job and is still bragging about the service and price, there is no better recommendation. Tell the contractors who recommended them, when you make an appointment for an estimate.

How Do I Judge Shingles?

Shingles used to be graded by weight. This is no longer the case. Never-the-less, better shingles, have longer warranties and weigh more than inexpensive shingles. Standard shingles have 20, 25 and 30 year warranties. The most expensive shingles may have life-time warranties. Typically only the warranties on the most expensive shingles are transferable. Where permitted, there is usually a cost involved for warranty transfer.

The price of shingles is quoted per square. A square is the amount of shingles necessary to shingle a 10' x 10' area (100 square feet). Usually a 20% factor is added to the actual square footage for scrap, cutting and ridge caps.

Roofing

Many roofers consider a 20 year Warranty Organic shingle to be the equivalent of a 25 year Fiberglass. A 25 year Warranty Organic is often assumed to be the equivalent of a 30 year Fiberglass.

The greatest value of a Warranty is that it shows the faith the manufacturer has in the product. Most structural defects show up within the first two or three years. Americans sell their homes and move every seven years on average. Most Warranties are not transferable. Statistically, therefore, most warranties are invalid for a minimum of two thirds of the warranty period. Improper attic ventilation destroys shingles and will also invalidate the warranty.

How Much Should Labor Cost?

Roofers often figure estimates using a price per square that includes labor and materials. This price varies with the size and difficulty of the job.

Where Should I Shop?

The average large discounter or lumber yard will often have prices that are two to five dollars per square less than the roofing specialist. However, the big boxes are usually one man bands. They carry a limited selection of shingles by a single manufacturer. If another manufacturer offers a lower price tomorrow, you can bet your last quarter they will switch. In the event you need a bundle of replacement shingles after the switch, you will be out of luck.

Currently the shingle of choice at the big boxes is Owens Corning. This is an excellent fiberglass shingle. Some discounters carry a relatively good selection of Owens Corning in 20, 25, 30 year warranty and even dimensional shingles in a limited range of colors.

Roofing wholesalers are specialists. They tend to have more displays and literature. They have the time and talent to give you helpful hints and do a little more hand holding than the average mass merchant.

Many wholesalers track which color of a specific shingle was shipped to a particular building site. So if you are considering a major premium shingle purchase, such as IKO Renaissance XL dimensional shingles in a green slate color, they can tell you where you can drive by and see an entire house roofed in your selection.

How Do I Shop for Shingles?

Shop for the shingles you want first. Then, ask the shingle wholesaler for recommendations on roofing companies. The wholesaler will usually be glad to give you the names of several roofers in your area he believes will do a good job with his shingles. Call them all out for a quote. Tell them that they were recommended by the wholesaler. Ask for references of other roofing jobs they have done, preferably with the same style of shingles you want. Don't be content to just call the references. Drive by and make sure you like the workmanship.

What Else Does My Roof Need?

In high ice and snow environments, like the North East, Northern, and Great Lakes Regions, snow and ice shield should be installed under the shingles and Building Paper covering the final three feet of roof line extending to the drip edge. I also recommend snow and ice shield on top of all flashing around the chimney and vents.

Depending on their condition, the decking, soffit and gutters may need to be replaced. The condition of the decking will not be known until the old shingles are torn off. However, you should know about projected decking, soffit and gutter replacement costs before the contract is signed.

Gutters come in both vinyl and aluminum. The biggest benefit of aluminum is that it is possible to get seamless gutters. Frankly, vinyl gutters used to be inferior. However, the new Snap Seal vinyl gutter has more tensile strength and much greater weight bearing ability than either aluminum or the old fashioned vinyl gutters. Snap Seal gutters are available through most full service roofing suppliers.

What Should Be Specified in the Contract?

The estimate and contract should include the exact dimensions of your roof; the specific make, name, identification number, warranty and color of shingles you are buying; the make and names of soffit vents, ridge vents, any other roof vents, or number and name of roof ventilators; the name and style of roofing underlayment; snow and ice guard; manufacturer and style of gutters (if they are being replaced); and cost per foot of deck or soffit if replacement is needed.

The contract should also include a completion date and penalty clause if work is not finished on time; schedule of payments, never pay more than a third down; and cost and timeliness of trash clean up and removal. This is especially important if the old shingles need to be torn off.

What about Insurance?

Workman's compensation & liability insurance is especially important. Roofing is a very dangerous occupation. Many homeowners have lost their homes because a worker was injured on site and the contractor was not

Roofing

insured. If injury or property damage is caused on the job, you, the homeowner, may be liable for hundreds of thousands of dollars in workmen's compensation or liability claims.

I know that I have talked about contracts in other chapters. However, it doesn't hurt to be repetitive when the information can save you everything you own.

It is very important that you receive certificates of insurance directly from the roofer's workmen's compensation and liability companies before work begins.

Do not accept a photo copy of an existing certificate of insurance. The coverage may have been terminated. Also check with your homeowner's insurance agent to see if you should have extra protection during the job.

Is There Any Way I Can Extend the Life of My Shingles?

If your shingles are just old, but in fair condition, and your budget is not quite ready for the cost of re-roofing, consider coating the shingles with a waterproof shingle repair coat like Roof Guardian by ORD (Oregon Research and Development Corporation). Call for information and the dealer nearest you[3].

---

[3] See Appendix for Supplier Phone List.

Roofing

This type of fix costs about half the cost of re-shingling and adds about 7 years to the life of your shingles. It is definitely noticeable and I would not recommend it if you are in the process of selling your house.

How Do I Know If I Can Add Another Layer of Shingles?

If there is only one layer of shingles on a roof, you can safely add a second, in some municipalities even a third layer of shingles is allowed, before a complete tear off is required. After two layers of shingles it's been a minimum of thirty or forty years and it is a good idea to do a complete tear off just to see what the decking looks like.

Chapter 17
Siding

Siding

What Is It?

Technically siding can be anything you put on the exterior walls of your house, but since this is a book on upgrading your house, you already have made your choice of sidings. That means that this chapter is on what you should use to side a room addition, or what you should select to re-side your entire house.

If you already have brick or stone siding, you are going to keep what you have. If you have shingle, wood panel, T 1-11, aluminum, steel, or vinyl siding, you may be considering something else.

Today, the most popular siding placed on room additions or older homes is vinyl siding. Most people who change their home's siding, change it to vinyl. Most people who have a room addition sided, have it sided in either T 1-11 or vinyl.

What choice is best for you. If you have a fifty or a hundred year old house in an area of similarly aged, well maintained houses, you would be advised to keep to your original siding, unless all the other houses in your area are going the vinyl siding route.

In this respect vinyl siding is a great deal like swimming pools. You don't want to have the only house in the neighborhood with a swimming pool, or the only house in

Siding

the neighborhood without a swimming pool. Standing out either way can strongly effect your homes resale value.

If you have a relatively new home, keeping in step with the neighbors is not such a consideration.

I would like to stress that painting is an excellent alternative to re-siding in most circumstances. I even wrote a book entitled **Take the Pain Out Of Painting - Exteriors-** that covers painting any and every kind of exterior surface, in great detail.

Aluminum or Vinyl?

If you don't want to re-paint, re-side. Now, which should you choose: aluminum or vinyl siding? The original siding of choice was steel or aluminum siding. Aluminum had a price advantage over steel, so it took the lead.

The original aluminum and steel sidings were excellent products. Aluminum and steel will last forever. And PPG Tedlar and DuPont Imron coatings had been developed for the military and wore like iron.

Funny thing, when manufacturers sell a product that lasts forever, nobody has to come back in five or ten years to get it replaced. Every sale eliminates a customer. It didn't take long for the boys in the back room to discover that a product that good could be bad for business.

Siding

The decision was obvious. Soon, new, improved (from the sales point of view) siding products appeared with cheaper paint that started looking bad after ten or fifteen years. Unless you happened to be a homeowner, life was good.

It turns out that aluminum and steel siding also dented when accidentally hit by something (like a baseball) and siding would actually crimp as a house settled. Although paint companies have come out with special products that make repainting aluminum and steel siding a breeze, but nothing can be done about denting. You can't take a dented house into the bump shop. Dented siding has to be replaced.

Vinyl siding came on the scene. It had several advantages. It was cheaper than aluminum and just bounces back when dented. Moreover, since vinyl's color is not a coating, but an integral part of the material itself, it can't be scratched or wind blasted off.

Vinyl is softer than metal, however, so it can be pitted and worn down by the natural grit in the wind over years, and colors can gradually bleach in the sun. Manufacturer's research has greatly improved vinyl's resistance to fading over the years and that should no longer be considered a major drawback. Dark colors are still vulnerable. Buying brown is just asking for trouble.

Siding

Vinyl comes in just about every design that natural wood comes in. The various wood grain patterns are very realistic. One caution with wood grain patterns. They look beautiful, but the pattern tends to hold dirt. Smooth stays cleaner, longer. If you use wood grain vinyl, be prepared to clean it regularly.

Can I Clean Vinyl & Aluminum Siding Myself?

Sure you can. Manufacturers like Aluminu and Armorall have developed special vinyl and aluminum siding cleaners that you just spray on with a garden hose, agitate, and rinse off. The Detroit Quality Brush Co. (DQB) has developed a long handled, curved edged, siding brush that is perfect for this job.

How Can I Tell if Vinyl Siding Is Good Quality?

All vinyl sidings are not created equal. If a quote comes in that is a good deal lower than the rest, be suspicious. Good quality vinyl panels have about the same reflective quality as an eggshell paint and are at least .040" thick. High quality is .045" thick. Anything in between should wear well.

Siding

Other good clues to the quality of vinyl siding are the length and guarantee against color degradation in the Warranty. Properly installed, vinyl siding is not going to fall apart, so the signal of the manufacturer's confidence in its product is strength, or weakness the Warranty's protection against fading and discoloring.

Most of these Warranties are not transferable, so the probability is that you will have moved before fading is noticeable.

Any Installation Tips?

Siding is becoming more DIY friendly all the time, but windows are a problem area. It is very easy to screw up and the mistakes stick out like sore thumbs. My advice, learn all you can before you do.

Check out the siding installation video tape by Home Time. Better still, volunteer to help a buddy do his. Practice on his house before doing your own.

Siding

Can I Trim Out Vinyl Siding in Vinyl, Or Do I Have to Use Aluminum for the Fine Details?

More and more trim pieces are being constructed in vinyl. Installers can not get extra thick, .05" panels for underneath the soffits. But realistically, your installer is going to have to trim out some of the pieces around windows or bay areas in aluminum.

How Do I Paint Vinyl Siding?

Painting vinyl siding is easy. Many manufacturers has developed special paints for painting aluminum and vinyl siding. Just make sure that you:

1. Clean thoroughly before applying paint.

2. Always work in the shade. Start early in the day and work around the sun. Never paint in the direct sunlight. The heat retained in the vinyl can ruin the job.

3. Apply enough paint. You want to apply two thick coats that will dry to at least a 5 mill finish.

See my exterior painting book for other tips.

Siding

Anything Special I Should Look out for When Getting an Aluminum or Vinyl Siding Quote?

The quotation procedure is the same as we have discussed throughout the book. Go to wholesale siding suppliers to get to know all about the different types of siding and get the names of installers they recommend. If you use the Winter for planning and checking referrals, you can be one of the first on the contractor's Spring list.

With aluminum or vinyl siding, you want to see a job that are currently under way if possible. Look to see how well the wrap has been placed around the house and how meticulous the alignment is.

You also want to see jobs that are four or five years old so that you can speak to the owners and see if they had any problems or call backs.

Chapter 18
Walks & Drives

Walks & Drives

Most Common Types

The four most common types of walks and driveways are loose, asphalt, concrete, and concrete pavers.

Loose stone or tile drives last only a few years before heavy maintenance is required. If properly maintained, asphalt can last ten to fifteen years before retopping is necessary. A good concrete drive should last fifteen to twenty years. Pavers should last at least fifty years, but maintenance will be required due to root growth, water channeling, and winter freeze and thaw cycles.

Prices are roughly proportionate to longevity.

Loose Fill

Loose fill walks and driveways are composed of crushed stone, tile, or aggregate. Their big plus is that they are cheap. The big minus is that they are cheap. They require constant maintenance, develop ruts easily, can create a lot of dust during the summer, and are very difficult to keep clear of ice and snow in Northern climes.

Repair and maintenance is relatively easy. As holes develop, you get another load of crushed stone, tile or slag, and start shoveling.

Walks & Drives

Loose fill drives are fine out in the country, but not used much by us city folk.

Asphalt

Asphalt walks and drives are made of bituminous materials in what is called a hot mix. Installation requires heavy equipment.

All asphalt is not created equal. Shady characters can lay down, who knows what, and the resulting drive will not last much longer than it takes your check to clear.

All asphalt is made of three different ingredients: stone, sand, and the bituminous material that glues everything together, asphalt. The strength of asphalt is determined by the size of the stones and the proportion of stone to sand to bituminous materials.

When constructing a road or driveway, asphalt is layered over a sub-base. The depth and quality of the sub-base is the key ingredient to the longevity of the paving material. This is true for any paving material, asphalt, concrete, or pavers.

When the sub-base of an asphalt job is laid the base is made up of crushed stone, highway gravel, recycled road, or crushed concrete. The thicker, the better the sub-base, the longer you can expect the drive or road to last.

Walks & Drives

Automobile traffic is immaterial. According to industry professionals, one semi-trailer causes the road bed more strain than a thousand cars. The asphalt we drive over on highways is called a highway mix and is designed to stand up to very heavy truck traffic.

Highway mix asphalt is composed of a high percentage of large stones, filled in by sand, held together by bituminous materials. It has a relatively rough surface and is not as dark as driveway asphalt.

Commercial grade asphalt is designed for driveways and light duty parking lots. It is composed of smaller stones and a higher proportion of sand and bituminous material to give a smooth, dark black appearance.

The difference in the cost of materials between highway and commercial grade asphalt, is only one or two dollars a foot. However, the equipment required to do the big highway jobs costs a million or more dollars, while the equipment needed to lay commercial grade asphalt is (only) in the hundreds of thousands of dollars.

Realistically, this means that no contractor is going to be willing to lay highway grade asphalt on your 500 square foot driveway, unless he happens to be paving your street and has a little extra time.

Walks & Drives

A good residential asphalt driveway will have 5 or more inches of stone, aggregate, or gravel sub-base, topped by 4 inches of asphalt. The asphalt will be laid in two, 2 inch "lifts (layers of asphalt)." The minimum acceptable residential drive should have a five inch deep sub-base and two one and one half inch lifts (three inch total).

Generally, the depth of the lift is double the size of the largest stones in the asphalt mix. That means a two inch lift, could have one inch diameter stones. A one and one half inch lift, could only have three quarter, quite often only five eighths, inch stones.

Remember, the larger the stones, the thicker the base, the longer lasting the job. You will get many years of extra use out of the higher priced product.

How Much Should an Asphalt Driveway Cost?

The price of an asphalt driveway is directly connected to the distance the product has to be hauled from the asphalt factory. In general terms, you could figure $3 to $4 a square foot for commercial grade (residential) asphalt. If your are a long way from the asphalt factory, the price may be increased 50¢ to $1. per square foot or more.

Walks & Drives

There Are a Couple of Stones Showing in My Driveway. Is The Job Ruined? What Should I Do to Fix It?

Forget about it. Remember what I said about the size of the stones being half the thickness of the layer of asphalt. A stone showing, just means that two stones landed on top of each other when they were pressed into place.

This isn't a defect in the job. Pulling out the stone could effect the integrity of the surface, so leave it alone.

Does Asphalt Need to Be Sealed?

Asphalt roads, drives, and walks are a lot like chewing gum. As long as you are chewing it, it is very elastic. Stop chewing it for a couple days and it becomes stiff and brittle. Residential walks and driveways need to be sealed because there is not enough traffic on them. Asphalt highways do not need to be sealed because the continuous pounding of the traffic keeps them supple.

This doesn't happen on a low traffic walk or driveway surface, so coating with a good water base emulsion sealer keeps the asphalt from oxidizing and protects it from oil and transmission fluid leaks.

Walks & Drives

How Long Should I Wait?

Manufacturers say sixty days. Most asphalt pavers like to see the asphalt season for a year before the first seal coat.

Do I Need to Seal the Driveway Every Year?

No. Too much sealer can build up on the surface and make the asphalt lose traction. The best plan is to seal the driveway every two to three years, depending on wear.

How Do I Seal My Asphalt Driveway?

Materials needed: Bix Driveway Asphalt Cleaner, Quikrete Professional Cold Patch, Asphalt Emulsion Sealer like Alco Heavy Duty Emulsion Sealer or Sealcrete MasterSeal II.

Equipment needed: Blower, Brush, Trowel, Long Handled Brush or Squeegee.

A thorough cleaning and application of sufficient sealer to do the job are the two most critical steps in sealing asphalt.

1. Clear all debris from the drive by brushing or blowing. If you have a lot of dried mud, etc., wash it off and let dry thoroughly.

Walks & Drives

2. Neutralize any oil or transmission fluid stains with a petroleum neutralizer like BIX Driveway Asphalt Cleaner.

3. Fill any cracks of indentations with Professional Cold Patch by Quikrete. Trowel on then tamp down. If the cracks are over one half inch wide, or wide and deep, upgrade to Gator Pave. Gator Pave is much heavier duty and can be used year round. It even adheres in water.

4. Apply the Alco Heavy Duty Asphalt Base Emulsion Sealer or Gibralter Sealmaster MasterSeal II with a brush or squeegee. Do not use a roller, it will make the coating too thin. You have to get a lot on.

5. Reseal about every two years.

Which Is Better, Cold Tar Emulsion Sealer or Asphalt Emulsion Sealer?

Both are good products. The cold tar emulsion sealer builds up and promotes checks or reflective cracking. These cracks are really just cracks in the sealer, but they are unsightly.

Asphalt emulsion sealers are more expensive, but they do not build up, promote check or reflective cracks, and are very black. The rich black color is highly prized by home owners.

Walks & Drives

My Asphalt Drive Has A Lot of Cracks and Some Alligatoring. Does It Have to Be Replaced?

No one wants to replace a driveway any sooner than necessary. If your asphalt driveway has a great many cracks and a few ruts, ask contractors for an estimate on just topping off the drive with an inch and a half layer of new asphalt.

Many homeowners try to economize by only having a one half inch thick coat applied. That is very poor economy. Remember, the asphalt is twice the thickness of the stone. A one inch lift of asphalt can only have 1/2" stone. A 1 1/2 inch thick lift of asphalt can have 5/8" to 3/4" stone. The larger stone makes a much longer lasting job.

Beware of asphalt crews who knock on the door and say they are in the neighborhood and can give you a "real good price" on adding a new layer of asphalt or sealing the drive.

It could be the best deal in town. It could also be a con to get your deposit check or they may just spray a fine layer of oil on your drive which has absolutely no benefit.

Get references and check out the contractor big time before you let loose of a single dollar bill.

Walks & Drives

Concrete

Since concrete driveways can last fifteen to twenty-five years or more, you probably have never shopped for one before. Here are a few pointers.

First, decide whether you really need a new concrete drive or walk. The driveway surface can look terrible, yet the concrete may be structurally sound. Replacement may not be necessary.

Four Methods to Fix

There are four methods of concrete repair short of total tear out and replacement: back filling and sealing, leveling, resurfacing and repouring.

Filling and sealing is cheap and brings back the integrity, but may leave the walk or drive looking like it has a bad case of the zits.

Leveling costs 1/3 to 1/2 the cost of a new drive or walk. It will bring the original slab up to grade, but will not do a thing about the appearance of the drive.

Resurfacing makes a drive or walk look like new and saves you 30 to 50%.

Repouring is the final alternative. It means you need to tear out and replace the entire job. If your drive is severely cracked, it may be the only alternative.

Walks & Drives

Filling & Sealing

Materials needed: Mason Sand, Backer Rod, Alcoguard, Quikrete, Mr. Mac, Sikaflex or Eucolastic Crack Sealer.

Equipment needed: Small Shovel, Ice Chopper, Scissors.

Fill small, thin cracks under 1/2" in width, with a ready to use crack sealer. Just snip the top and pour. The crack sealer acts like an expansion joint.

Many crack sealers or fillers are black like traditional expansion joints. Alcoguard is considered one of the best of these. If you don't want the black lines, both Quikrete and Mr. Mac's make gray, concrete crack sealers. Sikaflex and Eucolastic make caulk like products. If you have a large area to cover, a product like Alcoguard can be the most cost effective.

When the cracks are 1/2" or wider, water will have washed a channel under the concrete. Back fill these with mason sand and tamp down with an ice chopper. Repeat the process several times. Mason sand does not clump like ordinary sand. Fill the last 1 1/2" in depth with a backer rod and crack sealer.

Walks & Drives

Concrete Leveling or Mud Jacking

If the concrete has heaved, or sunken, or tree roots have pushed the drive out of level you can save the cost of replacement by using a mud jacking, or concrete leveling, company. The company drills 1 1/2" to 1 3/8" holes in the concrete, and forces a sand and sub soil mix under the slab, refilling all the voids where the sand has been washed away and lifting the slab to its original position.

By the time the concrete leveling company has finished, the drive, patio or walk will be as level as the day it was poured. This "fix" is usually good for at least five to seven years. After the drive has been leveled, fill all the fine cracks with crack sealer, and all the wide cracks with backer rod and crack sealer.

Resurfacing

If the concrete has settled and broken in several areas, you can often use the old concrete drive as a foundation and repour a three or four inch bed over the old surface. If you choose this, make certain that the contractor has a good track record with this type of work.

You don't have to settle for just a plain sidewalk look. You can resurface it and beautify your property, by calling in a resurfacing specialist that will cover the sur-

Walks & Drives

face with a bonding coat, then apply a thin resurface coat that can be formed into patterns and tinted to look like pavers.

Pouring New Concrete

If you decide to pour a new driveway, the concrete should be at least four inches thick. Actually, the thicker the better. If you are going to park a heavy truck on the driveway, or have an in-home business and get occasional deliveries from a semi-trailer, or have any type of truck traffic heavier than a light pickup truck, increase the thickness of the slab to six inches.

The composition of the concrete used in the drive should be a 5 1/2 to 6 bag mix and contain 5% to 8% entrained air. Entrained air is a fancy name for those little air pockets that give concrete the flexibility to withstand freeze/thaw cycles.

The concrete mix should have what is called a four to five inch slump. The slump is a measure used by professionals to determine consistency. A four inch slump is preferred. A five inch slump is the maximum permissible. To get an idea of what this means, imagine filling a coffee can full of concrete, then turning it upside down like you were building a sand castle.

Walks & Drives

At first, the pile of concrete would be twelve inches high. After about fifteen minutes the pile might have spread out and only a height of eight inches. Subtract eight from twelve and you get a four inch "slump".

When the concrete is poured you want as little troweling as possible. Making a driveway extra smooth, makes it slippery and destroys traction.

If the driveway will receive heavy traffic, it is a good idea to reinforce the six inch depth with mesh. While the new fiber reinforced concrete is excellent for patios and walks, the extra strength of metal mesh is still preferred for driveways.

Pricing

If you have an existing drive, removal of the old concrete will usually take a day and cost between fifty cents and a dollar (1997 prices) per square foot. This cost can vary greatly depending upon the complexity and size of the job.

The average size of a driveway is 16' foot wide by 30' long and can be prepared and poured in a day. The cost for a laying a four inch thick slab is usually $1.75 to $2.50 per square foot. Mesh or fiber reinforcing is extra. The additional cost for fiber reinforcing is usually eight to ten cents a square foot additional. The cost for mesh is approximately ten cents a square foot.

Walks & Drives

Speaking from personal experience, I believe that expansion strips are critical to the survival of concrete driveways. The average contractor will run a vertical, fiber filled, cut down the center of the pad. I suggest adding several horizontal relief cuts as well as angular relief cuts where the driveway meets the garage and at the end of the driveway apron.

How Can I Protect the Job?

Materials Needed: Thompson's Ultra

Equipment Needed: 2 Gallon Fruit or Deck Sprayer.

Once the job is done, the best way to assure a long lasting walk or driveway is proper maintenance. Don't just protect the driveway. Seal all walks, steps, porches.

Let the concrete cure for sixty days. Then hose off the driveway. Let it dry overnight and apply the sealer the next morning while the concrete is still cool. Application is very easy. You can use a 2 gallon sprayer and lay down a good thick coat.

Two of the best water stop sealers are Thompson's Ultra in the blue container or Ducksback Sealer.

Do not use their all purpose sealer because it costs a little less. You want the Ultra. Also, do not try to do an extra good job by using an expensive acrylic sealer. It will make the surface too slippery.

I Have a Brand New Home. Can I Use the Same Sealer for Sealing the Driveway and the Garage Floor?

Materials needed: Water Base Acrylic or Emulsion Sealer.

Equipment needed: Pail, Large Roller, Long Roller Handle.

The garage floor never gets rained on, but it sure does have a lot of the elements attacking it, road salts stuff like that. Buy a high quality clear Water Base Acrylic or VOC Emulsion Concrete Sealer. When you pour it out of the container it will look milky. It goes on milky so that you can see it, then turns clear as it dries.

If you've gone to a couple of places and they don't have a water base, they will usually have a zylene base acrylic cement sealer. In the garage that is okay, just don't pick the hottest day of the year to do it. The zylene is going to make you feel like your head just came off of your shoulders and it is going to smell real bad in the house even though you did it in the garage. You roll this material on with a paint roller and a long handle stick.

Walks & Drives

Acrylic and emulsion sealers are a lot more expensive than the water sealers you put on the driveway. But they hold up really well against hot car tires, road salt, and chemicals.

Unfortunately, it builds a film and shows everything so you are going to have to keep the garage a lot cleaner. It is not like the water seal you use on the exterior. When "Thompsons" dries you can't tell you have a sealer on until it rains. An acrylic sealer looks wet. That means it refracts light, so any imperfections in the floor show up big time.

Pavers:

Pavers make an elegant statement and are almost indestructible. They cost a great deal more than concrete but can last fifty to a hundred years.

Their greatest strength is also their greatest weakness. Because they are imbedded in sand or slag, not cemented together, pavers move with freeze/thaw cycles and almost never crack. Because they are not cemented together they can shift with the seasons, requiring regular maintenance to remain flat.

Walks & Drives

Either you are going to have to become very good at pulling out errant pavers, leveling and tamping down the slag, then putting in new sand and repositioning the pavers yourself, or you are going to have to resign yourself to calling in the paving contractor ever year or two to have the errant pavers put to right.

I have a paver patio. I love the look. I call the company every other year.

Can I Build My Own Paver Drive, Walk or Patio?

Yes you can. It is very hard work, but more and more D-I-Y'ers are doing it. All the big paver companies have very good instruction brochures, run workshops, some even have videos. My **Complete Deck & Paver Guide** also gives complete, step by step directions.

Look at a lot of paving jobs, attend a lot of seminars, read books, watch videos, and talk to a number of people who have actually done this kind of a project before you decide to do it.

Should Pavers Be Level?

No, pavers, like concrete, should always be laid on a slight slope so that water naturally drains away from the pavers and away from the house. If a normal slope for concrete would be 1" every 10 feet, it would be 2" every 10 feet for pavers.

Walks & Drives

Do Concrete Pavers Need to Be Sealed?

No/Yes. Paver manufacturers first told us that no maintenance was necessary. Technically, they told the truth. However, sealed pavers have, what they call, the "wet look." It makes the pavers look like they have just been rained on. The colors are darker and the stones retain a slight sheen. Altogether, it is a great look. Sealing the pavers, also seals in the sand in which they are placed. This keeps the sand from being washed away as rapidly.

What about Pricing?

Pricing varies greatly around the country. In Canada, they use a great deal mover pavers than we do in the United States and the price for an equal paver job is 30 to 50% lower than in our most competitive markets.

Here in the US, prices are more competitive in Detroit and Chicago than in many other parts of the country. Keep in mind that at least 50% of the cost of a paver job is labor. The higher the labor cost, the more expensive the job will be.

This also means that the shrewd D-I-Y'er who does the work him or herself will save a minimum of 50% off the prevailing local rate. They will also have found that this is very hard work on the knees, shoulders, and back.

Walks & Drives

Fabulous Fakes

Paver are so "hot" right now that a number of "almost as good as" alternatives have been developed. They give the paver look, without the paver price.

The Quickrete Company, and several others, have developed, low cost forms for walk ways that allow you to lay down a form and pour in your own concrete. These are fine for small patios or walks.

For big jobs, some concrete specialists will lay down a layer of concrete and form it to look like pavers. Now, at least one asphalt company is doing the same thing with asphalt drives.

If you have a big driveway that has cracked, but you don't like the idea of having to pay to get all the old concrete broken up and pulled out and new concrete poured, you can resurface it (like I discussed in the Resurfacing portion of this chapter) in a multitude of different paving styles, textures and colors, by calling in a resurfacing specialist, like Concrete Technologies Incorporated.

This procedure can be used anywhere that you have concrete, So you can let your imagination go a little bit wild and make any drive, walk, patio, or even a garage floor look like it is pavers.

The company covers the existing concrete surface with a bonding coat, then applies a thin resurface coat.

Walks & Drives

The final result looks exactly like pavers. You can call their national headquarters[1] to see if they have licensed a contractor near you.

If you need a new drive or patio, companies licensed and trained by Stampcrete Decorative Concrete[2], will come out to your home, tint the fiber reinforced concrete just before it is poured, then hand stamp the still wet cement into your choice of designs using highly specialized Stampcrete tools. Design choices range from Fieldstone and Slate, to Wood Plank, to Mexican and South American Tiles, as well as the traditional Brick and Cobblestone paver designs.

The Concrete Technologies and Stampcrete products are concrete looking like pavers. Their special paver looks are priced at a substantial premium over poured concrete, but a good deal less than true pavers. They have the same strengths and weakness that poured concrete has vis a vie pavers. That is, while no single "paver" will shift during frieze/thaw cycles, slabs of concrete are still subject to the cracking.

The newest faux paver look, doesn't involve concrete. If you like the feel, and the pricing of asphalt, but want the look of pavers, you are in luck. Integrated Paving Concepts Inc.[3] has developed a process called Street Print Pavement Texturing. This process makes an asphalt road or driveway look like it was made of pavers in your choice of an off-set brick, soldier course, herringbone, or decorative arch design.

---

[1] See Appendix for Supplier Phone List.
[2] Ibid.
[3] Ibid.

Walks & Drives

Street grade asphalt is laid, textured, then bonded and sealed, and a colored epoxy modified acrylic coating is added. The procedure takes heavy equipment, so it cannot be used in backyards or on small jobs. The surface is warranted for three years, but the job will probably not need to be touched up more than once every five years.

Keep in mind, all these processes call for major investments by the concrete or asphalt contractor. If there is one in your market that is doing this, your lucky, it is an alternative you should consider.

Final Thoughts

Final Thoughts

It's Been Good.

We've been through every part of your house together. I hope by now you feel, like I do, that we are friends. I'm the neighbor down the street, or the one you talk to across the backyard fence.

I'd like to end this book with a couple of words to the young families whose growing families and needs for space are prime ingredients in making this book necessary.

Do-It-Yourself projects make great family projects. Please get the kids involved. I know that it may actually take longer, but your son or daughter will appreciate their room more, and have higher feelings of self-worth, if they help you take down the old wallpaper and put up the new.

Your house is their home, too. If you are upgrading the kitchen or painting the living room, they should be in the thick of it. Oh sure, they will grumble. There are a million things they'd rather do. But I guarantee that the whole family will treasure the shared experiences.

I know there is a lot of work to be done and you are stressed for time. But sitting down and helping with homework, going to watch a little league game, going camping, or taking the entire family to devotional services, takes precedence over painting or plastering in my book any day.

Final Thoughts

So go on. Goof off a little. Your house will be here, and in approximately the same condition, twenty years from now. We build our families, moment by moment and day by day.

Thanks for spending some quality time with me.

Your friend,
Glenn Haege

Final Thoughts

Appendix

Manufacturer's Phone List

Product	Company	Phone N0.
Citristrip Adhesive Remover	Specialty Environmental Technologies	800-899-0401
Air Bear Media Air Filter	Trion	800-338-7466
Air Conditioning	Lennox	214-497-5000
Air Conditioning	Bryant	800-428-4326
Air Conditioning	Rheem	800-621-5622
Air Conditioning	Rudd	800-621-5622
Air Conditioning	York	717-771-6418
Air Conditioning	Heil/ Inter City Products	615-793-0450
Air Conditioning	Carrier	800-227-7437
AquaStar Hot Water System	Controlled Energy Corp.	800-642-3111
Avonite	"Avonite Inc."	800-4AVONITE
Bathtub Relining	Re Bath Co.	800-426-4573
Bi-Glass Window Conversion	"Bi-Glass Inc."	800-729-0742
Bondex Texture Paint	Wm. Zinsser & Co.	908-469-8100
Bullseye 1-2-3	Wm. Zinsser & Co.	908-469-8100
Cabinets	Conestoga Wood Specialties Inc.	800-722-0427
Cabinets	Merillat	800-575-8759
Cabinets	Kraft Maid	800-914-4484
Cabinets	Mid Continent Cabinetry	612-297-0661
Cabinets	WellBorn Cabinet Inc.	800-336-8040
Cabinets	Wood-Mode Cabinetry	800-635-7500
Certified Duct Cleaners	National Air Duct Cleaners Association	202-737-2926
Certified Production Directory	National Fenestration Rating Council	301-589-NFRC
Cobra Ridge Vents	GAF materials Corporation	800-688-6654
Combo Vents	Combo Vent Company	800-298-7610
Comfort Base	Homasote Co.	609-883-3300
Complete-Heat	Lennox	800-453-6669
Composite Window	Hoosier	800-344-4849
Corian	Du Pont	800-444-7280
Cover Stain Oil Based Stain Kill	Wm. Zinsser & Co.	908-469-8100
Diamond Brite Sealer	Diamond Brite	800-334-8388
Drylock Cement Paint	UGL	800-272-3235
Ductless Air Conditioning	Space Pak/Mestek Company	413-568-9571
Durock Cement Board	US Gypsum	800-USG-4YOU

DuroZone heating controls	Duro Dyne Corporation	800-966-6446
Electric Fireplace	Dimplex North America Ltd.	888-346-7539
Electronic Air Filter	Lennox	800-453-6669
Electronic Air Filter	Honeywell	800-332-1110
Electronic Air Filter	Carrier	800-227-7437
Electronic Air Filter	Rheem	800-621-5622
Electronic Air Filter	Rudd	800-621-5622
Envira Cushion	Fairway Tile and Carpet	248-588-4431
EqualizAir	Xavier Enerprises	313-462-1033
Fiberglass Insulation	CertainTeed	800-441-9850
Fiberglass Insulation	Owens Corning	800-GET-PINK
Fiberglass Insulation	Johns Manville	800-654-3103
Filterete Air Filter	3M	800-480-1704
Flushmate	Sloan Valve Co.	800-875-9116
Flushmate Equipped Toilet	American Standard	419-447-7515
Flushmate Equipped Toilet	Eljer	601-566-2363
Flushmate Equipped Toilet	Gerber	847-675-6570
Flushmate Equipped Toilet	Kohler	414-457-4441
Flushmate Equipped Toilet	Mansfield	419-938-5211
Flushmate Equipped Toilet	Universal	800-955-0316
Geothermal	Geothermal Heating Association	800-417-5555
Geothermal	Water Furnace International	219-478-5667
HRV: Heat Recovery Ventilators	Broan	800-548-0790
HRV: Heat Recovery Ventilators	Duro Dyne	800-899-8346
HRV: Heat Recovery Ventilators	Honeywell	800-345-6770
HRV: Heat Recovery Ventilators	Lennox	214-497-5000
Hydronic Heating	Heat Link USA	616-532-4266
Hydronic Heating	Vanguard Plastics	800-775-5039
Interior Storm Window	a.1 Technologies Incorporated	800-533-2805
Interior Storm Window	American Magnetite	800-624-8483
Kilz Oil Based Stain Kill	Masterchem Industries	800-325-3552
Kitchen and Bath Planning Kit	National Kitchen & Bath Association	800-401-NKBA
Marathon Water Heater	Rheem/Ruud	800-621-5622
Media Air Filter	Honeywell	800-328-5111
Microbial Test Kit	Sanit Air	248-879-0440
Mr. Mac	Macklanburg-Duncan	800-654-8454
Natural Gas Fireplaces	Heat-N-Glo	800-669-4328
Natural Gas Fireplaces	Hunter	705-325-6111
Natural Gas Fireplaces	Napoleon - Wolf Steel	705-721-1212
Natural Gas Fireplaces	FMI	800-888-2050

Paver Design Concrete Resurfacing	Concrete Technologies	800-477-6573
Paver Look Asphalt	Integrated Paving Concepts	800-688-5652
Perma White	Wm. Zinsser & Co.	908-469-8100
Renewal Replacement Window	Andersen	800-426-4261
Ridge Vents -Roll Vent 2	Benjamin Obdyke	800-346-7655
Ridge Vents -Cobra	GAF Materials Corporation	800-766-3411
Roof Guardian	Oregon Research and Development Corp.	800-345-0909
ScaldSafe AdapterKit	Resource Conservation Inc.	800-243-2862
Skuttle Model 216	Skuttle Mfg. Co.	800-848-9786
Soffit Vents	"Globe Building Materials Inc."	219-473-4500
Solatube Roof Window	Solatube North America	800-773-7652
Space Guard Media Air Filter	Research Products Corporation	608-257-8801
Stampcrete Decorative Concrete	Stampcrete	800-233-3298
Sun Tunnel roof window	Sun Tunnel	800-369-3664
SunPipe roof window	The SunPipe Company	800-844-4786
Super Strength Vinyl Patcher	Quikrete Companies	404-634-9100
Tilt Pac	Caradco	800-238-1866
Total One Water Based Stain Kill	Master Chem	800-235-3552
Trion electronic air filter	"Trion Inc."	919-775-2201
WALLMATE	DOW USA	800-441-4DOW
Water Heater	A. O. Smith	214-518-5900
Water Heater	State Industries	800-365-0024
Windows	Pella	800-23-PELLA
Windows	Caradco	800-238-1866
Windows	Andersen	800-426-4261
Windows	Marvin	800-346-5128
Wood and Vinyl Replacement Windows	Louisiana Pacific	800-299-0028
Zap Pac	Marvin	800-346-5128

Index

**Ask your retailer about the following
Master Handyman books**

Fix it Fast & Easy!
with a Little Help from America's Master Handyman, Glenn Haege

ISBN 1-880615-00-2
$14.95

DIY technology changes daily. Problems that would have been almost impossible to solve just a few years ago, can be fixed quickly and easily, today. Glenn Haege can show you how. He has been solving America's DIY problems on the radio for over 12 years. Now, the very best of these tips, are included in this collection of most asked "How To" questions.

Kathleen Kavaney Zuleger's Book Review column says:
"The book tells the easiest way to do many of the hardest cleaning and fix-up chores. Haege names names, and tells the reader which products will do the best job."

***The Bookwatch* says:**
"From handling mildew problems to revitalizing a deck and sprucing up furnitue, this book has hints others miss....It is these tips on common yet seldom-addressed problems which make this such an important home reference."

There are special sections on Cleaning, Walls, Floors, Exterior Cleaning & Painting, Furniture Renewal & Repair, Decks and Heating.

This book includes:
- **Solutions to mildew problems.**
- **How to get professional painting results.**
- **Easy ways to remove water rings from furniture.**
- **Furniture refinishing tips.**
- **Cleaning dingy aluminum siding.**
- **Plus Much, Much More.**

Bring Back the Beauty to your Hardwood Floors.

If you are one of the millions who have just discovered hardwood floors underneath their carpeting, or are thinking about installing hardwood in your home, this book can be a real life saver.

Glenn Haege's *Complete*
HARDWOOD FLOOR CARE GUIDE

How to Refinish & Care for Your Wood Floors

ISBN 1-880615-38-X
$6.95

Glenn Haege tells you all about hardwood, then gives four different ways to refinish floors, including one technique that will let you get the entire job done in a single day.

This book will show you how to:

- Save hundreds of dollars on hardwood or pine floor refinishing.
- Bring back the beauty to an old, lusterless wood floor in a single day.
- Get new, light weight equipment that makes it possible for any man or woman to refinish hardwood or pine floors.
- Decide which type of floor finish goes best with your life style.
- Select new, miracle finishes that are easy to apply, dry in hours, wear well and have almost no odor.
- Decide whether you want to wax or not wax your floors.
- Keep your floors looking their best.
- Solve all sorts of problems from bubbles and blisters to water and paint stains, even (ech) chewing gum.
- Live with, and love your hardwood floors.

409

Learn How To *Paint it Inside:*

TAKE THE PAIN OUT OF PAINTING

By
Glenn Haege

America's Master Handyman

−INTERIORS−

ISBN 1-880615-19-3
$14.97

Take the Pain out of Painting -Interiors-
by Glenn Haege

Even people who have been painting for twenty years or more tell America's Master Handyman, Glenn Haege, that they started painting faster, easier, and with better, more professional results after reading this book.

The Bookwatch says:
"Finally: a guide to interior do-it-yourself painting which follows a very simple yet information packed step-by-step format!...A very basic, essential home reference."

The Detroit News says:
"Haege makes it easy for anyone smart enough to lift a paint can lid... to solve a particular painting problem."

This one, power packed book contains the information you need to have a great looking job every time.

This book will show you how to:
- **Prepare a room so well you may not need to paint.**
- **Remove wallpaper and peeling paint easily and prepare a firm painting foundation.**
- **Paint even slippery surfaces like kitchen cabinets.**
- **Use special Stain Kill Paints to solve *impossible* painting problems.**
- **Make paint look like wallpaper, wood, and stone, in a fabulous 40 page "Faux Finish" section.**
- **Plus Much, Much More.**

Fast & Easy! © 1995 MHP
Outside:
Take the Pain out of Painting -Exteriors-
by Glenn Haege

Your home's exterior paint is all that protects your family's largest single investment from the elements. America's master handyman, Glenn Haege, shows you the easy, economical ways to give your house the protection it deserves.

ISBN 1-880615-15-0
$12.95

George Hampton of *The Booklist* says:
"Writing for paint retailers, contractors, and homeowners alike, Haege vends plenty of practical information organized into step-by-step procedures for everything"

Hormer Formby, the originator of Formby Finishes Says:
"Glenn Haege knows more about Paints and Products than anybody I have ever known."

This book will show you how to:
- Get the most for your painting dollar.
- Choose a painting contractor.
- Get rid of mold and mildew.
- Prepare the surface so the paint will wear like iron.
- Paint wood, vinyl, aluminum, concrete, log, shingles and all other exterior surfaces.
- Varnish or revarnish a log cabin.
- Paint, stain, or varnish exterior toys and furniture.
- Plus Much Much More.

First Aid for your pocket book.

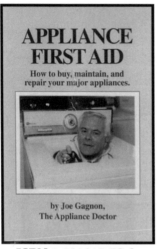

APPLIANCE FIRST AID
How to buy, maintain, and repair your major appliances.

by Joe Gagnon,
The Appliance Doctor

ISBN 1-880615-50-9
$14.97

This book is for you if you would rather spend your money on a new cd player than replacing the garbage disposer.

You don't get any medals for repairing or replacing a major appliance. *Joe Gagnon* shows how to keep them running better, longer; how to repair them when they break, and how to cut through the hype when it comes time to buy new.

The Chicago Sun Times says:

"Many Home Owners will save money with a copy of *First Aid From the Appliance Doctor,* by Joseph Gagnon. They also could save some lives."

The Davis Enterprise says:

"To become empowered, read appliance doctor's book."

TWENTYONE Magazine says:

"The information in *First Aid* can save you money. It's a book every homeowner will want to keep on the reference shelf."

This book will show you how to:

- Save hundreds of dollars on appliance purchase and repair.
- Cut through the lies in retail appliance ads.
- Tell the difference between a cheap promotional appliance and one that's built ot last.
- Make your appliances run better and last longer.
- Master the repairs you can easily do yourself.
- Keep from being ripped off on parts and service.

TO: **Master Handyman Press, Inc.**
P.O. Box 1498
Royal Oak, MI. 48068-1498

Please send me copies of the following books:
All books are sold with a 100% money back, satisfaction guaranty:

__ FIX IT FAST & EASY! 2   @ $19.95 each = $_____
__ FIX IT FAST & EASY!   @ $14.95 each = $_____
__ TAKE THE PAIN OUT OF PAINTING!
　　 - INTERIORS -   @ $14.97 each = $_____
__ TAKE THE PAIN OUT OF PAINTING!
　　 -EXTERIORS-   @ $12.95 each = $_____
__ Glenn Haege's Complete HARDWOOD
　　 FLOOR CARE GUIDE   @ $ 6.95 each = $_____
__ APPLIANCE FIRST AID
　　 by Joe Gagnon   @ $14.97 each = $_____

Total $_____

Michigan Residents: Please add 6% Sales Tax.

Shipping: Surface $3.50 for the first book and $1 for each additional.
Air Mail: $4.50 per book.

SHIPPING: $ _____

Total $_____

(See next page to order by phone or fax.)

Name: _____
Phone No _____
Address: _____
_____ ZIP:_____

Credit Card Information. Please fill out if you wish to charge.
Please charge my _____ Visa _____ Master Card
Expiration Date: _____ Card #_____
Name on Card: _____
Signature: _____

Four Easy Ways To Get More Master Handyman Books.

1. Ask your favorite book seller.

2. Charge by phone.
   Call 1-888-HANDY 81.
   (1-888-426-3981)

3. Charge by FAX.
   Fill out the Order Form on page 413 and FAX it to: 1-248-399-2636

4. Order by mail. Fill out the Order Form on page 413 and mail it to:
   Master Handyman Press, Inc.
   P.O. Box 1498
   Royal Oak, MI 48068-1498

TO: **Master Handyman Press, Inc.**
P.O. Box 1498
Royal Oak, MI. 48068-1498

Please send me copies of the following books:

All books are sold with a 100% money back, satisfaction guaranty:

__	**FIX IT FAST & EASY! 2**	@ $19.95 each = $_____
__	**FIX IT FAST & EASY!**	@ $14.95 each = $_____
__	**TAKE THE PAIN OUT OF PAINTING!**	
	- INTERIORS -	@ $14.97 each = $_____
__	**TAKE THE PAIN OUT OF PAINTING!**	
	-EXTERIORS-	@ $12.95 each = $_____
__	**Glenn Haege's Complete HARDWOOD**	
	FLOOR CARE GUIDE	@ $ 6.95 each = $_____
__	**APPLIANCE FIRST AID**	
	by Joe Gagnon	@ $14.97 each = $_____

Total $_____

Michigan Residents: Please add 6% Sales Tax.

Shipping: Surface $3.50 for the first book and $1 for each additional.
Air Mail: $4.50 per book.

SHIPPING: $ _____

Total $_____

(See next page to order by phone or fax.)

Name: _____

Phone No _____

Address: _____

_____   ZIP:_____

Credit Card Information. Please fill out if you wish to charge.

Please charge my _____ Visa _____ Master Card

Expiration Date: _____ Card #_____

Name on Card: _____

Signature: _____

Four Easy Ways To Get More Master Handyman Books.

1. Ask your favorite book seller.

2. Charge by phone.
   Call 1-888-HANDY 81.
   (1-888-426-3981)

3. Charge by FAX.
   Fill out the Order Form on page
   415 and FAX it to: 1-248-399-2636

4. Order by mail. Fill out the
   Order Form on page 415 and
   mail it to:
   Master Handyman Press, Inc.
   P.O. Box 1498
   Royal Oak, MI 48068-1498